JAPANESE RIFLES OF WORLD WAR II

Duncan O. McCollum

Published by Excalibur Publications, PO Box 36, Latham, NY 12110-0036.

ISBN # 1-880677-11-3   Third printing — May, 1998

Dedication

For Janet, whose enthusiasm and encouragement make everything fun.

Table of Contents

Introduction

Japanese small arms were held in low esteem for a number of years after World War II, probably because of the large numbers of crudely-made combat firearms and training rifles encountered in the final campaigns of the war and during the post-war occupation. Veterans of the vicious combat in the Pacific knew, however, that Japanese arms and equipment, although less sophisticated and technologically inferior to their own, served their purposes admirably. Still scorned by some collectors, Japanese rifles are simple and rugged, and proved highly effective in the hands of Japan's disciplined soldiers.

These rifles were the product of less than a century of intense modernization during which Japan was transformed from an agrarian, feudal society into a modern industrialized nation. In the early nineteenth century the most advanced firearms in Japan were matchlock muskets copied from those introduced to the Land of the Rising Sun by Portuguese traders in the mid-sixteenth century.

In an effort to eliminate corrupting foreign influences, in the 1630s Japan terminated trade with all nations except China and Holland. The limited trade with these two nations was conducted only at the port of Nagasaki. This situation lasted for over two hundred years, during which Japanese firearms technology did not change significantly.

The Japanese advancement from the matchlock began in the 1850s with the opening of Japan to international trade by American Commodore Matthew C. Perry. Soon Japan was importing various European rifles. In 1880 the first Japanese-designed rifle, designated the Type 13, was adopted by the military. Designed by Major Tsuneyoshi Murata, the Type 13 was a single shot 11mm blackpowder cartridge rifle, similar in many respects to the French Gras.

A later Murata design, the Type 22 (1889) rifle, kept pace with European firearms developments by using an 8mm smokeless powder cartridge and an eight-round tubular magazine located beneath the barrel.

During the years 1895-1898, development of a new rifle proceeded at the Koishikawa Arsenal in Tokyo under a commission headed by Colonel Nariaki Arisaka. The result was the Type 30 (1897) rifle, a five-shot weapon chambered for a new 6.5mm semi-rimmed cartridge developed in Japan. That rifle had a distinctive hook-shaped safety at the rear of the bolt from which it is occasionally referred to as the "hook safety" rifle. Japanese rifles from the Type 30 on are often generically referred to as "Arisakas" after the Colonel's leadership of this and a subsequent rifle design commission.

Arisakas and World War II

The Japanese manufactured over 6.4 million rifles and carbines in the 40 years from 1906 to 1945. Most of these rifles were still in use during the Sino-Japanese War of the 1930s and the Pacific War of the 1940s. During the war and subsequent American occupation of Japan, thousands of these rifles found their way to the United States as war souvenirs, making them one of the most common foreign military firearms available in this country today.

The World War II Arisaka rifles used a modified Mauser bolt action. It was the work of a second commission under Colonel Nariaki Arisaka, established in 1905, although Captain Kijiro Nambu actually designed the new action. Nambu was a prolific designer of military firearms, but is best known for his design of several Japanese service pistols and machine guns.

The improved Arisaka bolt action featured a hollow firing pin with an internal coil spring, a straight bolt handle, and a large, distinctive, round safety knob on the rear of the bolt. The bolt cocked on closing, was secured by two front locking lugs, and was one of the strongest military bolt actions ever produced. The safety was operated by

pushing the knob forward and rotating it about one-eighth turn to the right. Unlike other Mauser-inspired actions, the bulky safety knob of the Arisaka also served to deflect gases blown back as the result of a cartridge case failure or punctured primer.

This basic action was used on virtually all Japanese-manufactured combat rifles from the time of its initial adoption in 1906 until the end of World War II.

All Arisaka rifles featured Mauser style, five-round, staggered box magazines, and were loaded from stripper clips. There was no provision for a magazine cutoff such as is found on US Model 1903 rifles or on early British Lee-Enfield rifles. Most rifle and carbine models included long steel cleaning rods stored in a channel under the barrel. Rear sights on Arisakas had either a V-notch or a peep, and were adjustable for elevation only. By the middle of World War II a crude fixed peep sight was adopted for most rifles still being manufactured.

During the Second World War, the Japanese infantry was equipped with two basic models of Arisaka rifles. Until 1939 the standard arm, designated Type 38, was a long rifle with a 31-1/4" barrel, chambered for the 6.5mm cartridge. The Japanese retained the long rifle for infan-

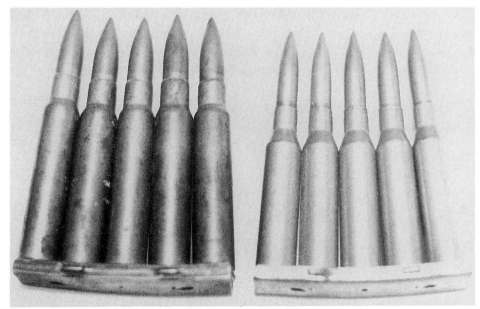

All Arisaka rifles were loaded from five round stripper clips. The 6.5mm cartridge, right, was used in the Type 38, Type 44, Type I and Type 97 sniper. The 7.7mm cartridge, left, was developed in 1938 and used in the Type 99 (long, short and sniper) and Type 2 paratroop rifle.

Rifle ammunition was provided to troops in cardboard boxes holding three loaded stripper clips. The star within the enclosed circle is the symbol of the 1st Tokyo Arsenal. The characters read "Type 99 Light Machine Gun Ammunition/Type 99 Ordinary Ball Ammunition/15 Rounds." This package contains machine gun loads, but is identical to packages in which 7.7mm and 6.5mm rifle ammunition was supplied.

try and short barreled carbine for cavalry long after other major military powers adopted a short rifle configuration suitable for use by all ground troops.

In 1939, the Type 99 rifle was adopted in both long and short form. These new rifles retained slightly-modified Arisaka actions, and were chambered for a new, larger 7.7mm rimless cartridge designed by the Japanese. Shortly after its adoption, the short version of the Type 99 became standard for all branches of the Imperial Japanese Army, and the manufacture of long rifles and carbines, including the Type 99 long, was discontinued.

This change in rifle models and calibers on the eve of World War II put the Japanese in the unusual position of fighting the entire Pacific War with two standard calibers of infantry weapons. At the time of the attack on Pearl Harbor, most of the Imperial Japanese Army was still equipped with 6.5mm Type 38 rifles and carbines, and Type 44 carbines. These had been used extensively in combat in China where Japan initiated hostilities in 1937. In the Pacific campaigns Allied troops encountered both Type 38 and Type 99 rifles in large numbers.

Most specialized rifle models — carbines, paratroop rifles, and sniper rifles — were simply design modifications of the basic Type 38 and Type 99 infantry rifles.

Many changes were made by the Japanese in the configuration and finish of rifle parts throughout the period 1906-1945. Heavy bombing of arsenal complexes during the latter part of World War II destroyed many production records, so information on production quantities and dates must often be extrapolated from observed serial numbers.

Parts variations and changes usually cannot be identified from records either, but can be placed in chronological sequence based on serial number observations. None of these relatively minor changes resulted in any change in rifle designation until 1943. That year the drastically-simplified Type 99 rifle was designated as the Substitute Type 99. These rifles are commonly referred to by collectors as "last ditch" rifles.

Markings on Japanese Rifles

Type Designation

The Japanese designated rifle models by the year in which they were officially designed or adopted for use. The Japanese character *shiki* is usually translated by Western collectors as "type" rather than "model."

The year of Type designation follows the Japanese, rather than the Western, calendar. The Japanese calendar begins with the traditional founding of Japanese culture in the Western year 660 B.C., and runs to the present. Adding 660 to a Western year converts it to a Japanese calendar year.

Additionally, the reign of each Japanese emperor was counted in years. Three emperors reigned during the late nineteenth and early twentieth century: Mutsohito, whose era is called Meiji (Bright Rule), 1867-1912; Yoshihito, whose era is called Taisho (Great Righteousness), 1912-1926; and Hirohito, whose era is called Showa (Enlightened Peace), 1926-1989.

Until the beginning of the reign of Emperor Hirohito in 1926, rifles (and other arms) were designated with the year of the current emperor's reign. Thus, the Type 38 rifle was designed in the 38th year of the reign of Emperor Meiji (1905), and the Type 44 carbine was adopted in the 44th year of his reign (1911). During the reign of Hirohito, rifles were designated by the last one or two digits of the adoption year according to the standard Japanese calendar.

Thus, the Type 99 rifle was adopted in Japanese calendar year 25**99** (1939), and the Type 2 paratroop rifle was adopted in calendar year 26**02** (1942).

The Type designation was stamped into the top of the receiver on most Japanese rifles using the character *shiki* for "type" and Japanese numerals.

Japanese character for *shiki*, usually translated as "type" and found stamped on the receiver tops of many Japanese rifles.

Arsenal Marks

Each Japanese rifle was marked with the symbol of the arsenal of manufacture or the arsenal that supervised the manufacturing subcontractor. This mark can be found on the left side of the receiver at the end of the rifle serial number. Rifles

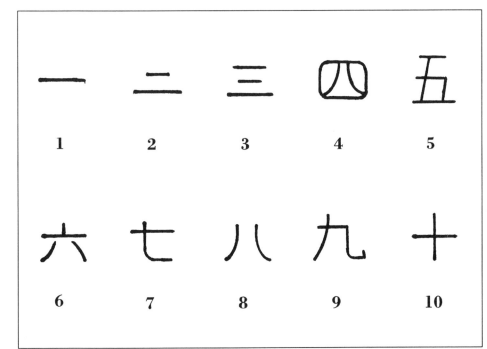

一	二	三	四	五
1	2	3	4	5
六	七	八	九	十
6	7	8	9	10

Japanese numerals for 1 through 10 used to designate rifle type.

Japanese Rifle Manufacturers

Symbol	Arsenal/Subcontractor	Period of Operation
	Koishikawa Arsenal (Tokyo)	1870-1935
	Kokura Arsenal	1935-1945
	Nagoya Arsenal	1923-1945
	Jinsen Arsenal (Korea)	1923-1945
	Mukden Arsenal (Manchuria)	1931-1945
	Toyo Kogyo	1939-1945
	Tokyo Juki Kogyo	1940-1945
	Tokyo Juki Kogyo	1940-1945
	Howa Jyuko	1940-1945
	Izawa Jyuko	1940-1945

manufactured by a commercial subcontractor bear the subcontractor's mark to the right of the supervising arsenal's mark.

Prior to about 1940, all Japanese rifles were manufactured at state-run arsenals. Three arsenals operated within Japan — Koishikawa Arsenal at Tokyo (1870-ca. 1935), Kokura Arsenal at Kokura in Fukuoka Prefecture, Kyushu (ca. 1935-1945), and Nagoya Arsenal at Nagoya on the southern coast of Honshu (1923-1945).

Rifle manufacture was transferred from Koishikawa Arsenal at Tokyo to Kokura Arsenal gradually during the early 1930s, and the same arsenal symbol was used by both facilities. The arsenal symbol for the Koishikawa (Tokyo)/Kokura Arsenal represented a stack of four cannon balls viewed from above. The symbol for the Nagoya Arsenal was a stylized version of two Japanese fighting fish head to head.

Two arsenals operated outside of the Japanese home islands — the Jinsen Arsenal at Inchon, Korea (1923-1945), and the Mukden Arsenal at Mukden, Manchuria (1931-1945).

Jinsen Arsenal was established by the Japanese in 1923 at Inchon as the Heijo Ordnance Factory. It operated under the supervision of the Koishikawa (Tokyo) and Kokura Arsenals until 1940, when it became the independent Jinsen Arsenal. The symbol for the Jinsen Arsenal is the Korean imperial symbol within a five-pointed star.

The Mukden Arsenal was built by the Manchurians and taken over by the Japanese in 1931 when they invaded and occupied Manchuria. The symbol of the Mukden Arsenal is a variation of that arsenal's symbol when it was operated by Manchuria prior to the Japanese takeover in 1931.

In 1939, when production of the Type 99 long rifle began, most of those rifles were made by the firm Toyo Kogyo (Oriental Manufacturing Company). Toyo Kogyo was located in Hiroshima Prefect in southwest

Honshu, and operated under the supervision of the Kokura Arsenal. It manufactured more military rifles than any other subcontractor.

Other commercial firms that manufactured rifles during the 1940-1945 period were Tokyo Juki Kogyo (Tokyo Rifle Manufacturing Company) located in Tokyo, Izawa Jyuko located at Osaka in south central Honshu, and Howa Jyuko also located in Osaka. Each of these firms operated under the supervision of the Kokura or Nagoya arsenals, and their rifles were marked with the supervising arsenal symbol followed by a unique symbol for the subcontractor.

Serial Numbers

All Japanese military rifles had serial numbers except extremely rare prototypes, other pre-production guns, and occasional rifles assembled very late in World War II. The serial number appeared on the left side of the receiver, followed by the arsenal symbol.

Initially, rifles made in Japanese arsenals were numbered consecutively within each Type designation. Over 2,000,000 Type 38 rifles were numbered in this fashion. During the late 1930s this scheme was replaced by a system in which rifles were numbered in blocks, or series, of 99,999. Each series was identified by a small Japanese character placed within a circle to the left of the serial number.

These characters, called *kana,* were taken from the 47 characters used by the Japanese to write non-Japanese words phonetically. The formal sequence in which *kana* are listed formed a short Japanese poem called IROHA (from the sounds of the first three *kana* — I, RO, HA). Collectors refer to individual series of rifles by the numerical position of each *kana* in IROHA. Specific blocks of *kana* were assigned to each arsenal or manufacturer to use for a specific rifle type. For example, Nagoya Arsenal manufactured Type 38 rifles in series

Series Markings

Series Number	Series Mark	Series Number	Series Mark
1	イ	24	ウ
2	ロ	25	キ
3	ハ	26	ノ
4	ニ	27	オ
5	ホ	28	ク
6	ヘ	29	ヤ
7	ト	30	マ
8	チ	31	ケ
9	リ	32	ラ
10	ヌ	33	コ
11	ル	34	エ
12	ヲ	35	テ
20	ネ	37	サ
21	ナ	40	メ
22	ラ	45	モ
23	ム		

ries 26-29, which are marked with the 26th through 29th *kana*.

Parts Numbering

Japan, like many European countries, numbered many parts on its rifles. Parts numbers ranged from 1 to 3 digits and were used to identify the components of individual rifles that had been fitted and then disassembled for batch processing. Numbered parts could be sorted and reassembled into the same units that were previously fitted together.

Until the 1930s, rifle parts were numbered to match a rifle's assembly number. The assembly number differed from the rifle's serial number and usually appeared on the bottom of the receiver, as well as on many small parts. During the 1930s, Japanese arsenals began using the last three digits of a rifle's serial number to match some parts, while others continued to be numbered to match a separate assembly number. After about 1940, the serial number was used almost exclusively for matching numbered parts.

Like most other major military powers, the Japanese arsenal system incorporated a program of refurbishing rifles. These rifles may exhibit multiple assembly numbers on the receiver bottom. Rifles whose parts were originally matched by an assembly number may be matched by the last two or three digits of the serial number after reworking at the arsenal.

Chrysanthemum

The sixteen-petal chrysanthemum is the symbol of the Japanese Emperor. It was stamped into the top of the receiver of Japanese rifles manufactured for the Imperial Japanese Army, and signified that the arm was the property of the Emperor.

At the end of World War II, the chrysanthemum was removed from most captured rifles by grinding, or was defaced with chisels, files, or other tools.

This mark appears below the chrysanthemum on the receiver of many rifles transferred to schools for training purposes.

Although definitive documentation of the reason and authority for the removal of chrysanthemums from rifles has never been reported, it is believed that the removal was performed mostly by the Japanese under American supervision after the surrender. It apparently was a face-saving gesture to allow the Japanese to avoid surrendering rifles bearing the Imperial symbol. Rifles captured in the field by American soldiers, (as compared to rifles captured in Japan at the end of the war), often have an intact chrysanthemum.

At various times, rifles were removed from military service and sold to other countries or transferred to Japanese schools as training weapons. Normally, the chrysanthemum on these rifles was overstamped with the Koishikawa (Tokyo)/Kokura Arsenal symbol or a ring of small circles to indicate that the rifle no longer belonged to the Imperial Japanese Army. Rifles given to schools often have an additional character stamped on the top of the receiver between the chrysanthemum and the type designation characters. Most of these "school-marked" rifles also have two or three zeros preceeding the serial number.

Type 38 Rifle

In the 38th year of the Meiji Era (1905), the Imperial Japanese Army designed an improved rifle that was adopted in 1906 as its standard infantry weapon. Its modified Mauser action, designed by Captain Kijiro Nambu, was one of the strongest military bolt actions adopted by a major country. The rifle was chambered for the same 6.5mm caliber cartridge that had been used in its predecessor, the Type 30 "hook safety" rifle adopted in 1897. In spite of its modern small-caliber bore, the Type 38 rifle retained the long barrel and straight bolt handle characteristic of most late nineteenth century infantry rifles. Japan did not follow Great Britain and the United States which had recently adopted short rifles with turned down bold handles that served both infantry and cavalry.

The top of the receiver was marked with the royal chrysanthemum and characters for "38 Type," reading from muzzle to breech. It had two gas escape holes located between the chrysanthemum and the type characters.

The barrel on the Type 38 was 31-1/4 inches long. Initially the rifling had six grooves, but later production guns had only four grooves. Under the barrel was a 29-7/16 inch steel cleaning rod secured by a stud that engaged in a groove near the front of the rod. The rod was removed by depressing a flat release spring located on the bottom of the stock immediately be-

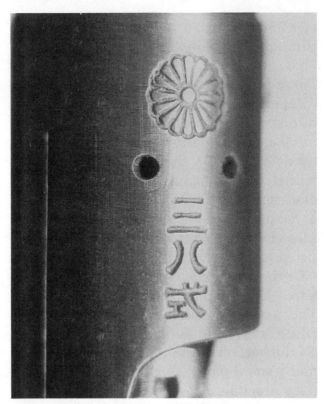

Reading from muzzle to breech, (top to bottom), the characters below the chrysanthemum on the receiver signify "38 Type."

hind the front band. When the rod was removed and the release spring depressed further, it disengaged the front band for removal.

The rear sight was a simple ladder graduated from 400 to 2,400 meters (later to only 2,200 meters) in 100 meter increments, and mounted at the top and rear of the barrel. There was no windage adjustment. The front sight was a tapered blade dovetailed into its base and usually secured with one screw or two pins.

A steel action cover, usually referred to

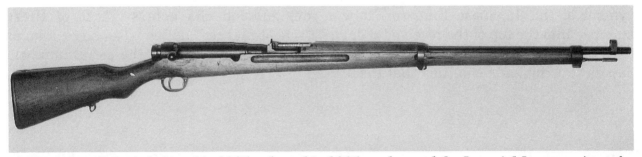

The Type 38 rifle was designed in 1905, adopted in 1906, and served the Imperial Japanese Army for nearly 40 years.

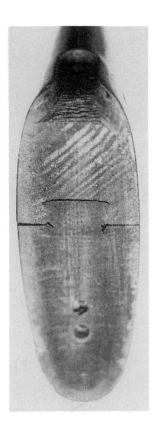

This view of the buttstock with buttplate removed shows how the characteristic two-piece Arisaka buttstock was dovetailed together.

as a dust cover, measuring 6-1/16 inches long fit into two grooves machined into the sides of the receiver and covered the entire action when the bolt was closed. Its purpose was to prevent dirt, rain, and other debris from entering and fouling the action. The bolt handle protruded through a hole in the dust cover and slid forward and back with the bolt as it was operated. The hole was elongated at the top and bottom to allow for the upward and downward motion of the bolt.

Type 38 dust covers had a small guide riveted or spot welded to the inside surface at the rear that contacted the bolt body just behind the bolt handle. Its purpose apparently was to prevent the dust cover from being pushed down against the receiver and binding.

The magazine was a Mauser-style internal, staggered box that held five rounds. It was loaded from stripper clips that were held in position by a guide machined in the front of the receiver bridge. The magazine follower was pushed upwards by a flat leaf spring. The magazine floorplate with attached leaf spring and follower was removed by pushing a grooved release catch located inside the front of the trigger guard.

Stocks were made of a soft, blond, Asian wood that was finished with a reddish brown varnish. The stock extended nearly to the muzzle, leaving 3-13/16 inches of the barrel exposed forward of the front barrel band. A separate wood handguard was trapped between the front of the rear sight base and the rear barrel band, covering the top of the rear half of the barrel. The wrist of the stock was strengthened with top and bottom tang pieces that ex-

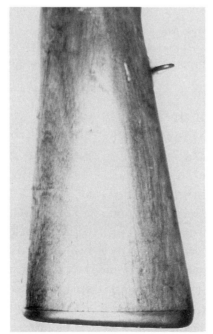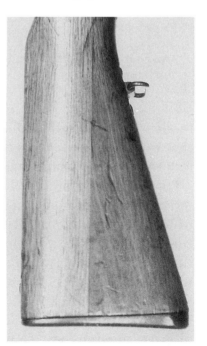

The flat metal buttplate, left, and the cupped variety, center, were used on most Type 38 rifles and carbines. The narrow cupped variant, right, was used on a limited basis on Kokura Type 38 rifles in the late 23rd and early 24th series.

Type 38 Rifle Production

Arsenal	Arsenal Mark	Estimated Quantity	Approx. Serial Number Ranges	Dates
Koishikawa (Tokyo); later Kokura		2,520,000	1-2,029,000 Series 20, 29,000-49,000 Series 22, 1-99,999 Series 23, 1-99,999 Series 24, 1-99,999 Series 25, 1-99,999 Series 26, 1-71,000	1906-ca.1940
Nagoya		313,000	2,021,000-2,031,000 Series 26, 1-99,999 Series 27, 1-99,999 Series 28, 1-99,999 Series 29, 1-3,000	1923-ca.1940
Jinsen (Korea)		12,000	1-1,000 Series 30, 1,000-12,000	ca.1939-ca.1940
Mukden (Manchuria)		117,000	1-38,000 5,000,000-5,065,000 65,000-79,000*	ca.1934-ca.1940

* Serial numbers in this range are preceded by two *hiragana* characters for "i" and "ro," the first two characters in the Japanese syllabary. These characters resemble "w" and "3," and these serial numbers have been previously misidentified as being in the 300,000 range.

tended to the semi-pistol grip. In spite of this reinforcement, the wrist was still subject to cracking from rough use.

The buttstock of the Type 38, like all Arisakas, was unique among military rifles in being fabricated from two pieces of wood that are dovetailed and glued together. The line between the two pieces was usually visible on the side of the buttstock and ran horizontally from just above the semi-pistol grip to the buttplate. This construction allowed the Japanese to use smaller stock blanks for their rifles and more efficiently use available wood. It also had the advan-tage of strengthening the toe of the buttstock because the grain of the lower piece ran parallel to the bottom edge of the buttstock. This reduced the possibility of the soft stock wood splitting at the toe.

The metal finish on most parts was a high quality hot blue that was a deep blue-black in color. Initially, certain small parts — trigger, rear sight spring, bolt release spring, and magazine floorplate release — were strawed; later they were blued. Early rifles also had bright bolts and cleaning rods; on later guns these parts also were blued.

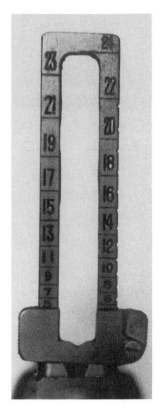

A rear sight with a v-notch and graduated to 2,400 meters was used on most Type 38 rifles.

A total of about 2,962,000 Type 38 rifles were manufactured at three arsenals in Japan, at the arsenal in the territory of Korea, and in occupied Manchuria. The rifles first were serialized using sequential numbers and later using the series system (see above). The accompanying table shows the approximate numbers of rifles manufactured at each arsenal, the serial number ranges, and the dates of manufacture.

Numbered parts initially were matched to an assembly number, and later by the last three digits of the serial number. All Nagoya and Jinsen Arsenal rifles were matched by serial number. Mukden Arsenal rifle bolts were marked with both the assembly number and the last three digits of the serial number.

Koishikawa (Tokyo) Arsenal rifles numbered sequentially were matched by assembly number, while series-marked rifles from the Koishikawa (Tokyo)/Kokura Arsenals were matched by a combination of assembly number and serial number. Some of the earlier Koishikawa rifles that later were arsenal refurbished may be matched by serial number.

During the approximately 35 years of its manufacture, many small parts and metal finish changes were made to improve the rifle. Although none of these parts variations resulted in a model designation change, they do reflect trends in the evolution of the Type 38 rifle. Significant changes were made in the buttplate, rear sight, front sight, bolt safety knob, rear sling swivel, rifling, and metal finish of certain parts.

Buttplates on all rifles except late Nagoya Arsenal production were flat metal, secured with a top and a rear screw. During the production of series 27 at Nagoya Arsenal, a cup-shaped buttplate was introduced. (A variant "semi-cupped" buttplate appeared on some rifles in series 23 and 24 produced at Kokura Arsenal.)

Rear sights changed significantly near the end of production at Nagoya and Mukden Arsenals. Until late in production all rear sights featured a V-notch. Beginning late in the 26th series production at Nagoya Arsenal, and above about serial number 5,060,000 at Mukden Arsenal, a peep aperture in a trapezoid-shaped sight

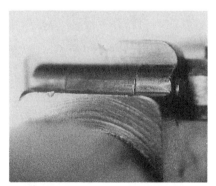  

The v-notch combat aperture was used on most Type 38 rifles and carbines. The peep in a trapezoid was introduced late in production at Nagoya (series 27 and 28) and Mukden (after about serial number 5,064,000) Arsenals. The semicircular peep was the final version produced at Nagoya and was introduced late in series 28.

Early production Type 38 rifles did not have front sight guards, top right, while guards were included on later production rifles and on all Type 38 carbines, bottom right.

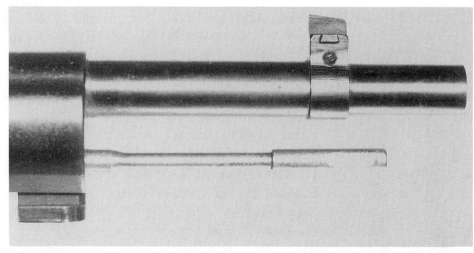

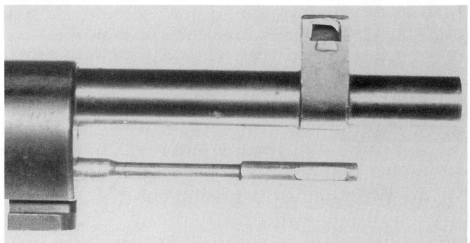

face was used.

In the later portion of the 28th series and in the 29th series produced at Nagoya Arsenal the peep was changed from the trapezoid shape to a semicircle identical to that used on the subsequent Type 99 rifle. On the trapezoid-shaped peep sights made at Mukden and the semi-circular peep sights made at Nagoya the elevation gradations were from 400 to 2,200 meters; all other production sights were graduated from 400 to 2,400 meters.

Front sights always consisted of a triangular blade held in a dovetailed base. Initially, the front sight blade was unprotected, but later rifles used guards on the front sight to protect it from damage. This change occurred at the beginning of the 22nd series at Kokura Arsenal. All Nagoya and Jinsen Arsenal and all but a few isolated Mukden Arsenal rifles had front sight guards.

Safety knobs in three different styles were

 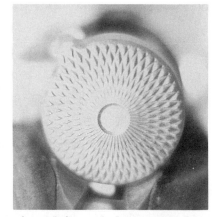 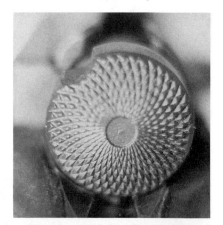

Type 38 safety knob variations are, from left, early large tang, later small tang, and the final notched variety. When the safety is rotated to the "safe" position, the tang or notch moves one eighth turn clockwise from the positions shown. The small tang and notched varieties also were used on the Type 38 and Type 44 carbines.

Type 38 Rifle Safety Knob Styles

Arsenal	Arsenal Mark	Approx. Serial Number Range	Safety Knob Style
Koishikawa (Tokyo); later Kokura		1-2,030,500, series 20 (early)	Large protrusion
		Series 20 (late)-23 (early)	Small protrusion
		Series 23 (late)-26	Notch
Nagoya		2,026,000-2,031,000	Large protrusion
		Series 26 (early)	Large protrusion
		Series 26 (late) - 27 (early)	Small protrusion
		Series 27 (late)-29	Notch
Jinsen		All	Notch
Mukden		All	Small protrusion

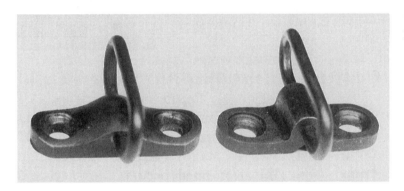

The two variations of rear sling swivel bases found on Type 38 rifles are the early smoothly-rounded type, left, and the later semicircle, right.

Arsenal rifles had an abrupt, protruding semi-circle through which the bail fit, similar to the style later used on Type 99 rifles.

Rifling on Koishikawa-produced rifles through about serial number 1,600,000 featured six grooves. Thereafter, all rifling had four grooves.

The metal finish on the bolt, cleaning rod, and several small parts changed during the period of production. Initially, bolts and cleaning rods were finished bright; later they were entirely blued. Triggers, sears, bolt release springs, and rear sight springs at first were strawed; later they too were blued.

Some Type 38 rifles had the numeral "0" stamped two or three times in front of the serial number. It has been suggested that these marks are connected with the transfer of rifles from military use to training use at schools since most of these rifles also had the school mark stamped on the top of the receiver.

used on the Type 38. The first variation featured a large protrusion on the left side of the knob's edge that pointed to the upper left when the safety was engaged by rotating the knob. Then, for a brief time a much smaller protrusion was used. Finally, late production rifles used a rounded notch in the edge of the knob as an indicator. The rear surface of all three safety knob styles was knurled, and the edge of large protrusion knobs was grooved, to facilitate rotation. The accompanying table shows the approximate serial number ranges using each variation of safety knob.

Rear sling swivel bases on most Koishikawa (Tokyo)/Kokura, and all Nagoya and Mukden Arsenal rifles had a smoothly-rounded profile, while those on Jinsen Arsenal and late 26th series Kokura

Type 38 Carbine

Production of the Type 38 carbine began at an undetermined time after rifle production to replace the Type 30 hook safety carbine for use by mounted cavalry and other specialized troops. The carbine had the same action as the rifle, an overall length of 38 inches, and a 19 inch barrel. A 17-1/4 inch cleaning rod was stored beneath the barrel and secured in the same manner as on the Type 38 rifle. The rear sight was a shorter version of the rifle sight with a ladder graduated from 400 to 2,000 meters.

To facilitate carrying by mounted troops, the sling swivels were mounted on the left side of the rear band and the left side of the buttstock. Like its full-length rifle counterpart, the carbine had a straight bolt and sliding dust cover, and was chambered for the 6.5mm cartridge.

Carbines were manufactured at the same government arsenals as the rifles, although in much smaller quantities. The accompanying table shows the approximate numbers of carbines manufactured at each arsenal, and their serial number ranges.

Numbered parts were matched to the serial number on Nagoya and Mukden Arsenal carbines. (Mukden bolts were numbered with both the assembly number and the last three digits of the serial number.) Sequentially numbered carbines produced by the Koishikawa (Tokyo)/Kokura Arsenals were matched to an assembly number, while the series 2 carbines from that

The short ladder sight of the Type 38 and Type 44 carbines was graduated to 2,000 meters.

arsenal were matched to either an assembly or serial number.

As on the rifles, several of the basic parts of the Type 38 carbines changed in configuration over time, although the carbine's official designation remained the same.

Buttplates were first flat metal and later the same cupped metal style as found on the rifles. All Koishikawa (Tokyo)/Kokura Arsenal and Mukden Arsenal carbines used flat buttplates; at Nagoya Arsenal the change from flat to cupped occurred in series 4 between serial numbers 12,000 and 15,000.

Front sight guards were included on carbines from the beginning of production.

Safety knob variations included only those featuring the small protrusion and the notch. All Koishikawa (Tokyo)/Kokura Arsenal and Mukden Arsenal carbines used the safety knob with small tang protrusion; at Nagoya Arsenal the change from small tang to notch occurred early in the 4th series.

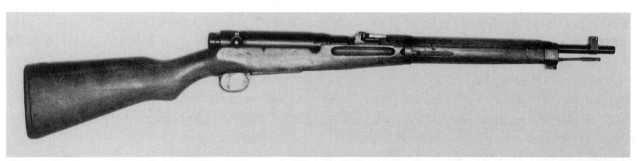

The carbine version of the Type 38 was intended for use by mounted cavalry or other specialized troops.

Rear sights on all Koishikawa (Tokyo)/ Kokura and Nagoya Arsenal carbines had the V-notch rear aperture. At Mukden Arsenal, a trapezoid-shaped peep sight similar to that found on late Nagoya Arsenal Type 38 rifles was introduced early in the 6th series.

As on the rifles, the metal finish on the bolt, cleaning rod, and several small parts changed during the period of production.

At Koishikawa (Tokyo)/Kokura and Mukden, bolts and cleaning rods were finished bright; at Nagoya these parts were blued beginning partway through the 4th series. Triggers, sears, bolt release springs, and rear sight springs were strawed on carbines produced by Koishikawa (Tokyo)/ Kokura and Mukden; after midway through the 4th series at Nagoya these parts were blued.

Type 38 Carbine Production

Arsenal	Arsenal Mark	Estimated Quantity	Approx. Serial Number Ranges
Koishikawa (Tokyo); later Kokura		292,000	1-212,000 Series 2, 12,000-92,000
Nagoya		206,000	1-2,000 Series 4, 1-99,999 Series 5, 1-99,999 Series 6, 1-4,000
Mukden (Manchuria)		45,000	1-2,000 600,000-628,000 Series 6, 28,000-43,000

Type 38 Cavalry Rifle

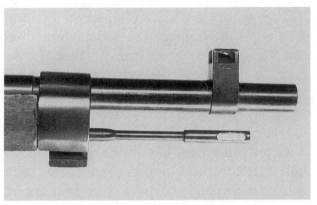

During the years 1940-1945 a shortened version of the Type 38 rifle was produced by converting existing long rifles. Collectors refer to this variation as the Type 38 cavalry rifle because it reportedly was produced for use by mounted troops. The rifle's receiver retained the original Type 38 markings, and there is no evidence that the Japanese referred to this rifle as anything other than a short rifle.

The cavalry rifle was produced by shortening the existing barrel to 25 inches and fitting it with a new handguard and shorter stock. A rod 23-1/2 inches in length replaced the original longer rod. The barrel was still held in place by two bands — a rear band that captured the front end of the upper handguard and included a bottom-mounted sling swivel, and a front band that included a bayonet lug.

The bolt, magazine, rear sight, and front sight were the same as found on the standard Type 38 rifle. Although cupped metal buttplates were used on many Type 38 rifles and carbines manufactured after the mid-1930s, and on the later Type 99 rifles manufactured during the 1940s, the cavalry rifle used a flat metal buttplate similar to that found on early Type 38 rifles and carbines. Also, despite its presumed cavalry role, the sling swivels were mounted on the bottom

Note the small step in the Type 38 cavalry rifle's barrel behind the front band. This step is from turning down the shortened barrel to fit the front band.

of the rear band and bottom of the buttstock, rather than on the side like both the Types 38 and 44 carbines and the Type 99 rifle.

When these rifles were reconfigured, many parts were renumbered to match the rifle serial numbers, which were not changed. A special assembly number and alignment marks were stamped in the bottom of the shortened barrel's breech end and on the adjacent end of the receiver. Other numbered parts may match the rifle's original assembly number.

Cavalry rifles are relatively uncommon and it is unknown how many were produced because they retain serial numbers from their original manufacture as full length infantry rifles. Apparently, all of the conversions were done at the Chigusa factory of Nagoya Arsenal.

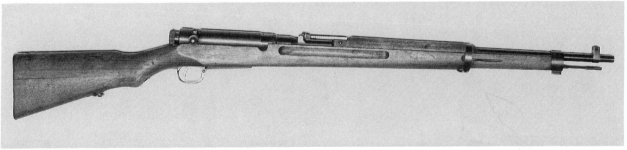

The Type 38 cavalry rifle was a full-length Type 38 rifle shortened and restocked for use by mounted troops. These rifles were not re-serialized, so it is unknown how many were made. They were produced in limited numbers during the 1940-1945 period.

Type 44 Carbine

In 1911 the Army adopted a modified version of the Type 38 carbine, designated the Type 44, for use by cavalry troops. It was manufactured concurrently with the Type 38 carbine from its adoption through the late 1930s.

The primary difference from the earlier carbine was the folding bayonet that was permanently affixed to the Type 44. The bayonet was attached with a massive steel housing that nearly encircled the muzzle end of the stock, shrouding the barrel forward of the front sight, and holding a locking mechanism and hooked quillon. The housing was secured to the stock with two round-headed screws.

The 15-3/4 inch long bayonet, (measured from the center of the pin on which it pivots), was roughly triangular in cross-section with a flat tip. The two lower surfaces of the blade were fluted, and the upper surface had a deep groove that ran its length. The blade was locked in its extended and stored positions by two large lugs on the bottom of the housing.

It was stored folded under the stock where it fit into a groove in the stock and rear band, and was released by depressing a large round press stud on the left side of the base of the blade. The hooked quillon was an extension of the large pin on which the bayonet hinged, and extended outward from its right side.

Because the storage location of the bayonet displaced the long cleaning rod of the Type 38 carbine, the Type 44 used a sectioned rod stored in a compartment in the buttstock. Two 8-5/16 inch rod sections and a jag tip were threaded for assembly. The small buttstock storage compartment was closed by a rotating plate mounted on the right side of the buttplate.

The bolt and magazine system of the Type 44 were identical to the Type 38, including the use of a sliding dust cover. The rear sight also was identical to that on the Type 38 carbine, and the front sight had raised guards. Sling swivels were mounted on the left side of the buttstock and rear band. The front swivel was angled to facilitate carrying the slinged carbine diagonally across the back of a mounted soldier. The buttplate was flat metal.

Approximately 91,000 Type 44 carbines were manufactured at the Koishikawa (Tokyo), Kokura, and Nagoya Arsenals between its adoption in 1911 and the adoption of the Type 99 rifle in 1939. Both sequentially numbered and series marked rifles were produced at each arsenal.

At Koishikawa (Tokyo) and Kokura Arsenals over 69,000 were numbered sequentially, followed by nearly 9,000 with series mark 1. At Nagoya Arsenal about 2,000 were numbered sequentially, followed by over 11,000 with series mark 2. It is unknown whether the Type 38 and Type 44 carbines were intended for use by different troops since both models were manufactured and issued simultaneously.

There are three primary variations of the Type 44 carbine recognized by collectors, although the rifle's official designation re-

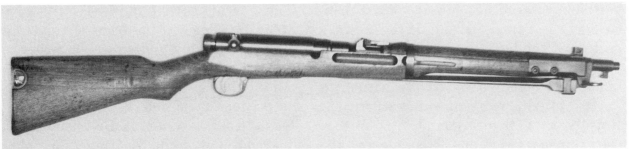

The Type 44 carbine is basically the Type 38 carbine design with a folding bayonet added.

23

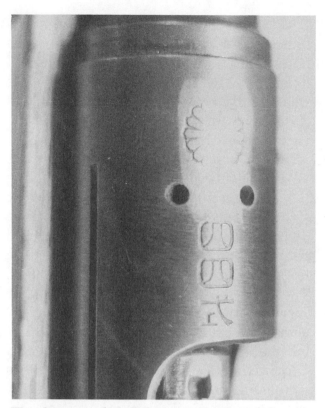

The characters below the partially-ground chrysanthemum read "4 4 Type" from the muzzle to breech (top to bottom). Surrendering a rifle with the Imperial symbol of the chrysanthemum intact was considered a great dishonor by the Japanese, so they were allowed to grind or deface the chrysanthemums on most rifles surrendered after the end of the war.

mained the same. These variations are based on changes implemented in the design of the bayonet housing. Initially, the housing was relatively short with the two attachment screws placed close together, and with a barrel shroud that fit tightly around the barrel.

This design exhibited two weaknesses: physical weakness of the link between housing and stock which could result in breakage of the forestock when excessive pressure was applied to the bayonet; and impairment of accuracy caused by the pressure of the barrel shroud on the forward portion of the barrel.

About 56,000 of these first variation carbines, numbered consecutively without a series mark, were manufactured at Koishikawa (Tokyo) Arsenal.

To remedy its strength deficiency, the

bayonet housing was redesigned to make it longer and more robust, with the screws more widely separated. At the same time the inside diameter of the barrel shroud was enlarged so that the barrel floated within the forestock, which solved the accuracy problems associated with the first variation housing. This style of bayonet housing is referred to as the second variation and was manufactured at the Koishikawa (Tokyo)/Kokura Arsenals between about serial numbers 56,000 and 65,500.

The housing was modified again by adding a small extension to its back edge to allow the rear securing screw to be moved a half inch farther back in the stock. This third variation was used until the end of production at the Koishikawa (Tokyo)/Kokura Arsenals and on all Nagoya Arsenal-produced Type 44 carbines.

As with Type 38 rifles, Type 44 carbines were sometimes factory refurbished. Some of the early variation carbines were upgraded to later configuration bayonet housings, and therefore, the bayonet housing variation may not conform to the expected serial number range.

Numbering of parts on Type 44 carbines spanned the transition from matching parts numbers to an assembly number stamped on the bottom of the receiver through the use of the last three digits of the serial number to match parts. Consequently, early production carbines are matched by assembly number, mid-range production by a combination of assembly number and serial number, and late production primarily by serial number.

Some carbines were marked with two or three "0"s added to the front of the serial number, possibly indicating transfer to schools for training purposes.

Metal finish was consistent throughout the production period at the Koishikawa (Tokyo)/Kokura Arsenals. Bolt bodies were finished bright, while the trigger, floorplate

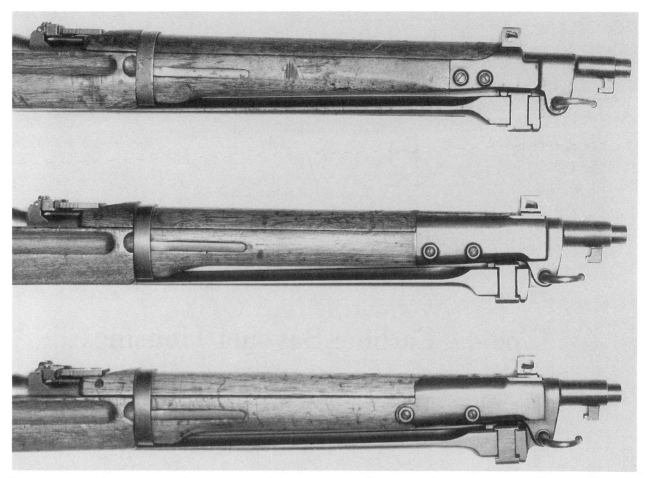

Three styles of bayonet housings were used during production of the Type 44 carbine. The smallest and earliest, top, was replaced by the sturdier second version, middle, and finally by the even-stronger third variation, bottom.

release, rear sight spring, and bolt release spring were strawed. The balance of the rifle was blued. This finish also was used for most of the Nagoya Arsenal Type 44 carbines. Late in production of the second series at Nagoya Arsenal, the small parts and the bolt were blued.

Several parts show minor changes in configuration during the production period. Safety knobs featured the small projection safety indicator until the notched safety was introduced late in series 1 at Kokura Arsenal and midway through series 2 at Nagoya Arsenal. Rear sling swivels throughout most of the production period had a gradual rounded profile to accommodate the bail, while very late production swivels had an abrupt semi-circle through which the bail passes.

The lightening holes in the front sight guards also were changed very late in the production period from an angled shape that mirrors the profile of the front sight blade to a rectangle with slightly-rounded corners.

Initial production at Koishikawa (Tokyo) Arsenal did not include drain holes in the stock. Later, two, and then three, 9/32-inch diameter drain holes were drilled in the bayonet channel on the bottom of the forestock. All Nagoya Arsenal-produced Type 44 carbines have two drain holes.

The internal configuration of the cleaning rod storage compartment in the buttstock changed between the first and second variations. First variation carbines had two unlined holes in the butt trap to hold two rod sections; later rifles had a metal-sleeved compartment that held both rod sections and the jag tip.

25

Type 44 Carbine Production

Arsenal	Arsenal Mark	Estimated Quantity	Approximate Serial Number Range
Koishikawa (Tokyo); later Kokura		78,000	No series, 1-69,000
		Series 1, 1-9,000	
Nagoya		13,000	No series, 1-2,000
			Series 2, 1-11,000+

Type 44 Carbine Bayonet Housings

Arsenal	Arsenal Mark	Estimated Quantity	Approx. Serial Number Range	Bayonet Housing Variation
Koishikawa (Tokyo); later Kokura		56,000	No series, 1-56,000	first
Koishikawa (Tokyo); later Kokura		9,500	No series, 56,000-65,500	second
Koishikawa (Tokyo); later Kokura		12,500	No series, 65,500-69,000+	third
			Series 1, 1-9,000	third
Nagoya		13,000	No series, 1-2,000	third
			Series 2, 1-11,000+	third

Type "I" Rifle

One of the more unusual Japanese rifles is referred to by collectors as the Type I, and was a hybrid of the Type 38 Arisaka and Italian Carcano. This rifle was designed for the Imperial Japanese Navy at Italy's Terni Royal Arms Factory. It was manufactured during 1938 and 1939 at the Royal Arms Factories at Gardone Val Trompia and Brescia, and at Beretta Arms. At that time, the small arms production of Japanese Army arsenals was completely absorbed by the Army, and the Navy was forced to acquire foreign manufactured rifles.

Contracts with the Italians called for supplying 60,000 Type I rifles to the Japanese. Although there is reported use of these rifles by Japanese Naval troops, they typically have no Japanese markings. The receiver is completely unmarked while the serial number appears on the left side of the barrel chamber. The lack of the royal chrysanthemum is perhaps indicative of these rifles' naval, rather than army, use. They were serialized in European style with a number preceded by a capital letter, A through N.

Although at least 14 letters have been observed in serial numbers, it is unknown how many rifles were manufactured within specific lettered series. The maximum within any letter series apparently does not exceed 10,000, and many series must consist of far fewer in order for the total number of rifles not to exceed the contract

The Type I used a Model 1891 Carcano-style bolt action, and its receiver lacked any Japanese markings, including the Imperial chrysanthemum.

number of 60,000.

The overall length of the Type I was either 49-1/2 inches or 50-1/2 inches. The difference was in the length of the buttstock, which on some specimens was shortened one inch by the Japanese from the length originally supplied by the Italians.

Interestingly, these stocks exhibit the same two-piece buttstock construction as all standard Arisakas. The cleaning rod was 28-7/8 inches long, one-half inch shorter than the Type 38 rod, reflecting the one-half inch shorter barrel of the Type I.

The Type I rifle was unique in several respects. It incorporated a Model 1891 Carcano-style action on a rifle that otherwise resembled the Type 38 Rifle and was chambered for the Japanese 6.5mm cartridge. The front sight (without protective guards), rear sight, front and rear bands,

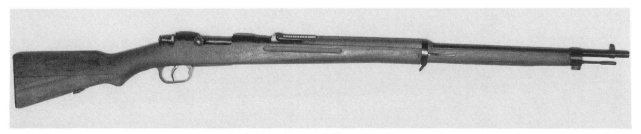

The Type I rifle was a unique blend of Arisaka and Carcano features. It was manufactured in Italy for the Imperial Japanese Navy in 1938-1939.

magazine, and rear sling swivel were virtually identical to the Type 38.

Differences included an oversized trigger guard, no top or bottom wrist pieces, and a buttstock that was more flat-sided and less rounded than the Type 38 stock. The buttplate, which was slightly rounded in profile, extended over the top of the buttstock only about 5/8-inch rather than the 1-5/8 inches of the Type 38.

The only other marks on these rifles consisted of Italian proof marks on the bolt and some internal parts. There was no assembly number and individual rifle parts were not numbered.

Metal finish of the bolt was bright or case hardened, triggers were blued or case hardened, rods bright or blued, while the balance of the rifle was blued. Light colored stocks were furnished to Japan unfinished, and many rifles remain in that condition today. Others appear to have been finished with an oil that significantly darkened the wood.

Type 99 Long Rifle

Japan's military experiences in Manchuria beginning in 1931 and China beginning in 1937 demonstrated that the 6.5mm rifle round was of insufficient power. In 1932 a 7.7mm semi-rimmed cartridge was developed and adopted for use in Japanese heavy machine guns. It was not until 1938 that a similar cartridge was proposed by the Army for infantry rifles.

That year experiments began at Futsu Proving Ground on new rifle designs of rifles using a rimless version of the 7.7mm cartridge. Recoil from the 7.7mm round was found to be too heavy in the experimental cavalry carbine, which was based on the Type 44 carbine, so design efforts focused on developing a full length rifle for infantry, and a short rifle for cavalry.

The Type 99 rifle was adopted in two lengths in 1939. The full length infantry rifle is called the Type 99 long rifle by collectors. It was manufactured in small numbers at only two facilities: Nagoya Arsenal, which produced about 8,000; and Toyo Kogyo, which produced about 30,000. Rifles produced at Nagoya were serialized without a series mark, while those produced at Toyo Kogyo were serialized with series mark 35.

The top of the receiver had a single gas escape hole centered between the royal chrysanthemum and characters for "99 Type," which read from left to right across the receiver.

The Type 99 long rifle had a slightly modified Arisaka bolt action, and retained the cupped buttplate and guarded front sight of late production Type 38 rifles. It continued the use of a partial upper handguard that protruded 5/16-inch forward of the rear band, and of the sliding dust cover. Virtually all other parts of the rifle incorporated design or functional changes from the Type 38.

The rear sight was a ladder type with a peep aperture resembling that on the latest production Nagoya Arsenal Type 38s, but graduated only to 1,700 meters. Added to the rear sight slide were folding wings intended to facilitate shooting at flying aircraft. With the sight ladder in the upright position, the wings folded down to project sideways from the sight and horizontal to the ground.

The wings were notched and marked along their length with the numerals 1, 2, and 3 corresponding to the estimated speed of the airplane in hundreds of knots. The notches or tip of the sight wings were used as a substitute rear sight aperture when sighting on a flying airplane in order to provide the proper lead to hit the aircraft.

A second change from the Type 38 was the addition of an 11-1/4" long wire monopod (measured from the bottom of the stock while fully lowered) attached to the bottom of the rear band. The rear band was fabricated with a rectangular block on its lower surface. A smaller square projection on the front of this block was drilled laterally for a hinge pin, on which the monopod pivots up and down. Two flat metal springs attached to the sides of the

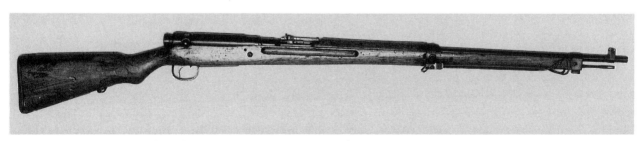

The Type 99 rifle introduced the 7.7mm rimless cartridge into Japanese service. The long rifle version, shown above, was made only briefly before being discontinued in favor of the short version.

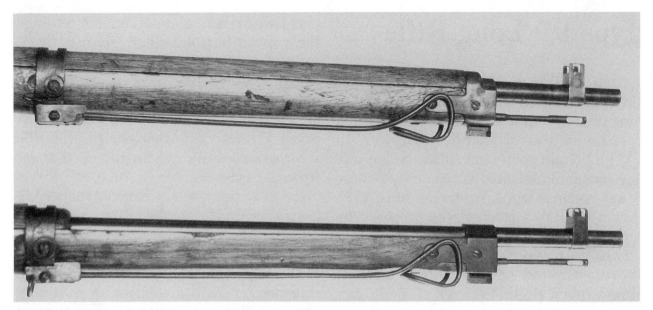

The Type 99 long rifle monopod, bottom, was one-quarter inch longer than that on the short rifle, top, and used a two-piece retaining spring rather than the one-piece spring on the short Type 99.

block provide pressure against the hinge and keep the monopod from flopping loosely.

In its lowered position the monopod was perpendicular to the ground and was intended to provide a stable support for the rifle when shooting prone. When folded forward, the lower end of the monopod gripped the forestock around the tangs of the front band and held it in its stowed position.

Originally, all Type 99 long rifles were issued with monopods attached, but most specimens are found without the monopod. Rifles no longer fitted with the monopod normally have three distinctive indentations in the stock wood immediately behind the front band caused by the monopod

gripping the stock when it was stowed.

The rear band, in addition to accommodating attachment of a monopod, was held in place by a bolt which passed completely through the band from the right side, went through the stock, and was secured in a threaded hole in the left side of the band. Raised reinforcing rings surrounded the holes in each side of the band, and its top is slotted as a lightening measure.

The front band also was redesigned from that of the Type 38. It was squared off on the lower and forward edges, and had 1-1/16 inch tangs that extended toward the rear of the rifle. A short machine screw passed through each tang and was secured

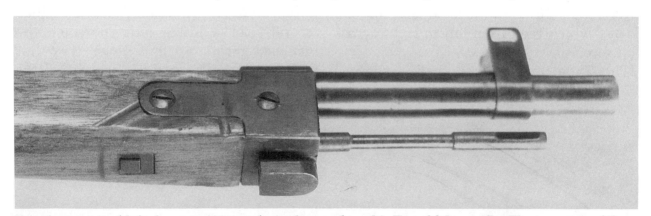

Use of a monopod left characteristic marks in the wood on this Type 99 long rifle. The presence of these marks on a long or short Type 99 indicates that a monopod was on the rifle at one time. Monopods are frequently missing from rifles that originally were equipped with them.

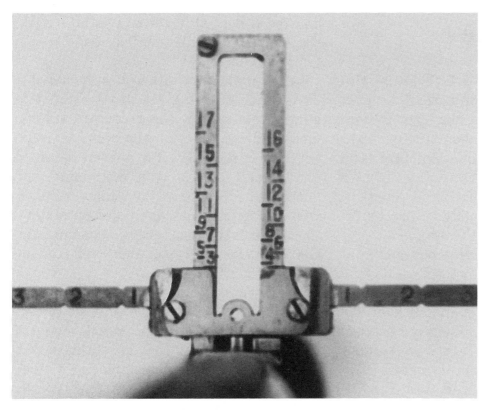

The anti-aircraft wings on the Type 99 long rifle sight are shorter and wider than those on the short Type 99, and have notches on both top and bottom.

stripping of the rifle. It was released by moving rearward a small catch located inside the top of the trigger guard.

The stock was similar to that of the Type 38 rifle with the addition of a 7/16-inch diameter transverse recoil bolt located below the receiver, and two 7/32-inch diameter drain holes. One drain hole was on the bottom, 3/8-inch forward of the floorplate assembly; and the other was on the right side above and just behind the recoil bolt.

Sling swivels were on the lower surface of the rifle, one attached to the rear band, and the other screwed into the bottom of the buttstock.

Overall, these rifles were very well made, with some of the finest metal finish found on any Arisaka. All metal parts were blued, except for the monopod springs, rear sight base spring and slide release catches, bolt release spring, and trigger, all of which were strawed.

internally to the cleaning rod locking mechanism inside the stock. A third screw passed through the main body of the front band from right to left in the same fashion as the screw holding the rear band. The front band incorporated the bayonet lug.

The cleaning rod was 29 1/4 inches long and was stored under the barrel as in previous models. However, the release mechanism was a small square press stud on the lower surface of the stock just behind the bayonet lug.

The magazine floorplate was hinged at the front to prevent its loss during field

Type 99 Rifle

The short version of the Type 99 rifle adopted in 1939 was originally designed as a cavalry rifle. After the Type 99 long rifle was discontinued, about 1940 or 1941, the short Type 99 became standard issue for all branches of the Army. It was longer than a carbine, and similar in length to the standard rifles already in use by the Americans, British and Germans.

The Type 99 rifle was produced in almost as great numbers as the Type 38 rifle, and is the most common model encountered by collectors. Approximately 2,497,000 Type 99 rifles were manufactured between 1939 and 1945 by a variety of government arsenals and private subcontractors.

Within this brief period, the Type 99 underwent more parts and configuration changes than any other Arisaka rifle, providing almost endless variations for collectors.

The Type 99, as first produced, incorporated several design features of the Type 99 long — monopod, anti-aircraft wings on the rear sight, hinged magazine floorplate, and recoil bolt. Other than overall length, the major visual difference was a full-length top handguard.

Early production rifles also included a 28-7/8 inch cleaning rod, front sight with guards, rear sight ladder graduated to 1,500 meters, drain holes on the right side and bottom of the stock, sling swivels mounted on the left side of the rear band and buttstock, cupped metal buttplate, receiver with a single gas escape hole centered on top between the royal chrysanthemum and characters for "99 Type," and chrome plated bore and bolt face.

When originally designed as a short rifle, the Type 99 was intended for issue to cavalry troops. Its rear sling swivel, mounted on the left side of the buttstock, was a large oval intended to accommodate a quick release cavalry sling. When the Type 99 became standard issue for all branches of the Army, the rear swivel was changed to the conventional oblong shape used on most other Arisaka rifles.

The monopod on the Type 99 was 11 inches long, (measured from the bottom of the stock while fully lowered), 1/4-inch shorter than that on the Type 99 long rifle.

During its production period, 1940-1945, the Type 99 rifle was simplified from its original configuration, top, to the crude Substitute Type 99 ("last ditch") variety at the bottom. Changes in many parts were implemented gradually, resulting in many variations of "transition" rifles, center. The sequence of changes incorporated by each arsenal or subcontractor was slightly different.

Type 99 Rifle Production

Manufacturer	Arsenal Mark	Estimated Quantity	Approx. Serial # Ranges
Nagoya Arsenal		1,088,500	No series, 1-99,999 Series 1, 1-99,999 Series 2, 2,500-99,999 Series 3, 1-99,999 Series 4, 10,000-99,999 Series 5, 1-99,999 Series 6, 1-99,999 Series 7, 1-99,999 Series 8, 1-99,999 Series 10, 1-99,999 Series 11, 1-99,999 Series 12, 1-1,000
Kokura Arsenal		592,000	Series 20, 1-99,999 Series 21, 1-99,999 Series 22, 1-99,999 Series 23, 1-99,999 Series 24, 1-99,999 Series 25, 1-92,000
Toyo Kogyo		557,000	Series 30, 1-99,999 Series 31, 1-99,999 Series 32, 1-99,999 Series 33, 1-99,999 Series 34, 1-99,999 Series 35, 1-57,000
Tokyo Juki Kogyo		41,000 57,000	Series 27, 1-41,000 Series 37, 1-57,000
Izawa Jyuko		32,000	Series 4, 1-10,000 Series 9, 1-22,000
Howa Jyuko		32,000	Series 9, 50,000-82,000
Jinsen Arsenal		94,000	Series 40, 1-94,000
Mukden Arsenal		3,000	Series 45, 1-3,000

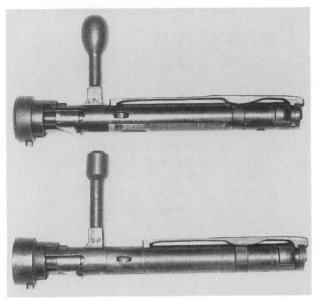

A plum-shaped bolt handle was used on all early configuration Type 99s, and through the end of production by Kokura Arsenal and by subcontractor Toyo Kogyo. The simplified cylindrical bolt handle and shorter extractor were used on late transition and Substitute Type 99 ("last ditch") rifles by Nagoya and Jinsen Arsenals, and by subcontractors Toykyo Juki Kogyo, Izawa Jyuko, and Howa Jyuko.

The flat spring on the rear band which held the monopod in position was a single piece of metal which wrapped around both sides and the rear of the block at the bottom of the band.

The front band, held in place with three screws, was rounded on its bottom edges to eliminate the sharp corners of the Type 99 long rifle front band.

Type 99 rifles were manufac-

Safety knobs. The knurled safety knob, top left, was used on all early configuration Type 99 rifles. The grooved version, lower left, appeared only on rifles manufactured from very late in Nagoya Arsenal series 6 to about two-thirds through series 7. The smooth variety, top right, appeared on some transition rifles produced by several manufacturers. Safety knobs on Substitute Type 99 ("last ditch") rifles usually retain a rough blob of weld from attachment of the shank, lower right.

tured by eight arsenals and private subcontractors in Japan, Korea, and Manchuria. Each arsenal or subcontractor was assigned one or more series marks to use in serializing its rifles.

Initial production at Nagoya Arsenal was without any series mark. Production of series 4 and 9 was divided between different manufacturers.

The accompanying table illustrates the manufacturer, manufacturer's mark found on the rifle to the right of the serial number, the approximate number of rifles manufactured, and the specific series produced by each manufacturer.

As World War II progressed, the Japanese ran short of strategic materials, including steel and wood for small arms. This, along with a need to increase production of rifles, led to a variety of parts changes in Type 99 rifles beginning about 1942.

By 1943 the rifle had been so altered that the simplified version was designated the Substitute Type 99 rifle, which remained in production until the end of the war in 1945. Rifles produced in the last two years

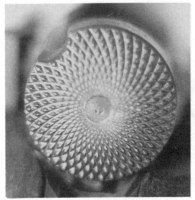

The characters on early Type 99 receivers read, left to right, "9 9 Type."

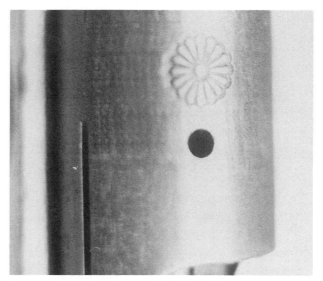

Later production Type 99 rifles did not carry any model designation on the receiver.

The small recoil bolt, top, was used on early configuration rifles at all arsenals, while Substitute Type 99 rifles used a large diameter bolt, bottom. The unusual square bolt, middle, appeared on a small number of rifles in the middle of Kokura Arsenal's series 24.

of the war exhibit rough metal finish with milling or lathe marks, rough welds, uneven bluing, poor fit of parts, and crudely-finished stocks.

The sequence of changes in major parts is described below, accompanied by tables indicating the series during which each major change was implemented. While the changes at all manufacturers inclined toward simplification, the sequence in which these occurred was not the same at each arsenal or subcontractor.

These parts modifications provide the collector with an almost unlimited variety of rifles when all the changes and manufacturers are taken into account. Although it is beyond the scope of this work to indicate every change, the major variations are described.

Bolt

Early production bolts have an oval or plum-shaped ball at the end of the handle, and a chrome-plated bolt face. Later bolts, except those produced by Kokura Arsenal and Toyo Kogyo, have a cylindrical handle, which at first was machined, and later rough cast. Chrome plating of the bolt face was eliminated midway through World War II.

Type 99 rear sights. From left: 1. Early sight with wings extended for use. The wings were intended to help soldiers obtain the proper lead when firing at a flying aircraft. 2. Unusual anti-aircraft sight wing extensions on a Kokura Arsenal series 22 rifle.

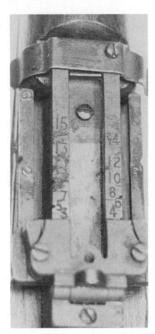

This row, from left: 1. Early configuration sight with anti-aircraft wings in the stowed position. 2. "Aleutian" sight. Rifles issued to troops in the Aleutian Islands included a sheet metal attachment to facilitate lifting the sight ladder while wearing gloves. 3. Early sight without anti-aircraft wings attached, an early transition feature. 4. Transition period sight without provisions for attaching anti-aircraft sight wings.

From left: 1. Short ladder sight used on most Nagoya Arsenal series 7 rifles. 2. Fixed peep sight found on most Substitute Type 99 rifles. 3. A variant fixed peep used on Jinsen Arsenal series 40 and some Nagoya Arsenal series 8 Substitute Type 99 rifles.

Extractor

Early extractors were 4-7/8" inches long, while late production extractors were 4-1/8 inches long.

Safety Knob

Early safety knobs were knurled on the rear face and appeared very similar to safety knobs on late Type 38 rifles. At one arsenal (Nagoya), the knurling was replaced with parallel grooves for a short time, while at other manufacturers the knurling was replaced by a smoothly-machined face. Late production safety knobs from all manufacturers have an irregular blob of weld on the face that remained from attachment of the shank.

Receiver Markings

All rifles had the royal chrysanthemum above the gas escape hole. Early production rifles had characters for "99 Type"

Rear bands. Top left: Band designed for attachment of a monopod. These bands were used on early transition rifles, even after use of monopods was discontinued. Rifles from Nagoya Arsenal series 5 and 6, Kokura Arsenal series 24, and Toyo Kogyo series 32 are often found with this style rear band, but assembled without monopods.

Center left: Rare monopod-style band not drilled for the monopod.

Bottom left: Non-monopod rear band with lightening slot in the top, often found on rifles in transition series.

Top right: Late, solid top band.

Bottom right: Extra-wide band found on the so-called Jinsen Special Last Ditch rifles, a variant configuration produced late in Jinsen series 40.

below the hole, while late production rifles did not have any type designation marking on the receiver.

Stock

Early configuration rifles featured full length handguards, finger grooves, drain holes below and on the right side of the receiver, and a small diameter (3/8-inch) recoil bolt. As production was simplified, one or both drain holes were eliminated (or in some cases filled), the finger grooves eliminated, and the top handguard shortened so that it projected only about 3/8-inch in front of the rear band.

On very late production rifles the stock forend is a separate piece of wood that is trapped between the two bands, and the recoil bolt is large — 25/32-inch in diameter. For a short time, Kokura Arsenal also used a square-shaped recoil bolt.

Occasionally, late configuration rifles are found assembled on previously-rejected early-style stocks. Inlets for early buttplates and front bands were sometimes filled before assembly with late-style parts.

Rear Sight

Initially, the rear sight ladder was 2-3/4 inches long and graduated to 1,500 meters. It included anti-aircraft sighting wings. The first step in simplifying production was to eliminate installation of the wings, although existing supplies of sight slides fabricated to accept wings were used until

Front band and sight variations. Top left: Early production rifle with front sight guards. The band was secured by three screws — one through the front and one from each side through the tangs. The later two-screw band used a single screw through the tangs.

Center left: The single screw band was used only on some series 9 rifles produced by Izawa Jyuko.

Bottom left: On Substitute Type 99 rifles, the front band had rough welds and was pinned to the barrel.

Top right: A flat-topped band was used on late Jinsen Arsenal rifles (series 40), referred to by collectors as "Jinsen Special Last Ditch" rifles.

Bottom right: Some early Tokyo Juki Kogyo series 27 Substitute Type 99 rifles were assembled on rejected early stocks already inletted for early style bands.

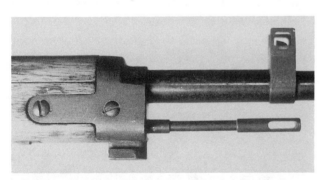
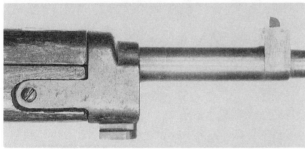
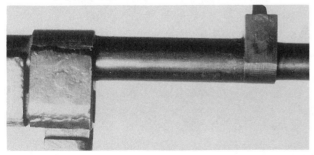
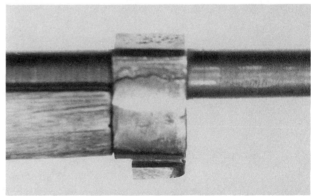
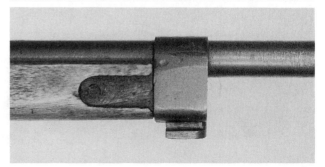

Rear sling swivels. The oval sling swivel, left, on some early "no series" Nagoya Arsenal rifles, was intended for use with a quick-release cavalry sling. The standard two-screw swivel, center, was used on most early and transition rifles. The single-screw variety appeared on Substitute Type 99 ("last ditch") rifles.

In some transition series one-screw swivels were installed in stocks already routed for two-screw swivels.

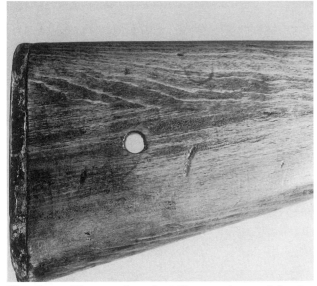

Very late rifles produced at Nagoya Arsenal (series 11 and 12) and by subcontractors Tokyo Juki Kogyo (series 27) and Howa Jyuko (series 9) had a hole in the buttstock for use with a woven rope sling.

exhausted. A later sight slide eliminated the fittings to hold the wings.

At Nagoya Arsenal a ladder sight with a shorter ladder 2-1/8 inches long, but still graduated to 1,500 meters, was used throughout most of the 7th series. Finally, Substitute Type 99 rifles had fixed rear peep sights zeroed at 300 meters. There are two different configurations of fixed peep sights.

Front Sight

All early production front sights had guards, while late production sights had an unprotected front blade.

Rear Barrel Band and Monopod

Early rear bands were slotted on top for lightening, had an asymmetrical sling swivel on the left side (wider at the top than bottom), and had the block on the lower surface for attaching the monopod. The first change in the band was to eliminate installation of the monopod, although existing supplies of monopod-style bands apparently were used up.

It generally is possible to determine whether a monopod was installed on a rifle by looking for the three distinctive marks in the stock behind the front band that were made by the monopod when it was closed. Later, the monopod attachment feature was eliminated from the bottom of the band, and the lightening slots were omitted from the top of the band. Late pro-

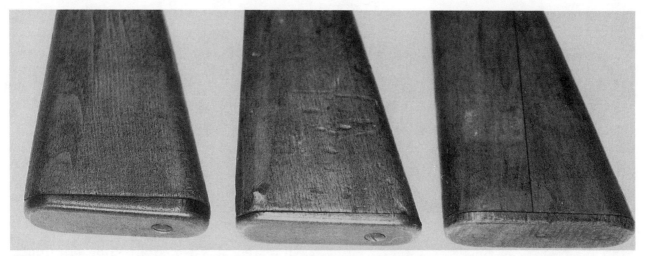

Early configuration and many transition Type 99 rifles had a wide, cupped metal buttplate, left, while Substitute Type 99 ("last ditch") rifles had a wood buttplate attached with nails, right. The narrow metal buttplate, center, appeared on rifles in the middle of Nagoya Arsenal series 7.

duction rear bands usually had a roughly-welded seam on the bottom surface.

Very late bands may have a patch spot-welded over the bottom seam, and may not have a sling swivel attached. There are over a dozen variations of rear bands, some of them specific to particular arsenals or subcontractors.

Front Barrel Band

Initially, the front barrel band was affixed to the rifle with three machine screws — one from each side through the tangs and into threaded holes in the cleaning rod catch mechanism, and one screw that passed completely through the band and stock from the right side and into a threaded hole on the left side of the band.

Later, when the cleaning rod catch was changed, a two-screw band was used in which both screws passed completely through from the right side to engage threads in the left side of the band. A single screw variation also was used by one manufacturer where the screw passed through the tangs.

On Substitute Type 99 rifles, the front band had no tangs, was welded together, and was pinned directly to the barrel, eliminating the need for screws.

Rear Sling Swivel

As mentioned earlier, initial production rifles at Nagoya Arsenal were intended as cavalry rifles and had a large, oval rear sling swivel for use with a quick-detaching cavalry sling. Most Type 99 rifles, however, utilized a parallel sided swivel secured to the stock with a two-screw base. On late production rifles the base was shortened and attached with a single screw.

Finally, a small number of extremely late production guns had merely a 3/8-inch hole drilled laterally through the buttstock to

A double-thick wood buttplate was used on a small number of rifles late in series 34 produced by subcontractor Toyo Kogyo.

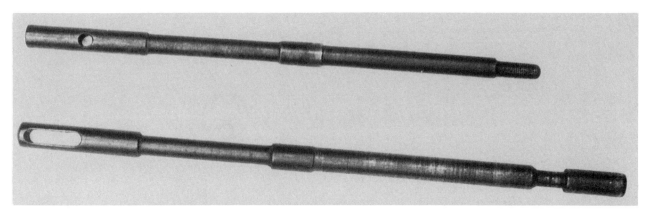

Short cleaning or stacking rods used on transition Type 99s: top, the 4-7/8-inch screw-in rod found on most transition rifles, and normally associated with a two-screw front band; bottom, an unusual 5-3/4-inch push-in rod found on a few Kokura Arsenal rifles from late in series 23 and early in series 24.

enable use of a simple rope sling.

Buttplate

Buttplates on the first Type 99 rifles were cupped sheet metal similar to those used on the late production Type 38 rifle. The widest dimension of the edge, at the bottom, was 1/2-inch. For a short period Nagoya Arsenal used a cupped metal buttplate with a narrower (1/4-inch) edge to save metal. Eventually, all manufacturers used a wood buttplate secured by three (later, only two) small nails.

Cleaning Rod and Rod Catch

Rifles first were issued with cleaning rods 23-3/4 inches in length. These were released by depressing a small, square catch release located on the bottom of the fore stock just behind the front barrel band. As yet another metal-saving expedient, mid-war rifles were equipped with a 4-7/8 inch cleaning or stacking rod. This short rod screwed internally into a round metal plug located where the square catch was located on earlier rifles. A few rifles in the late 23rd and early 24th series produced at Kokura Arsenal had a 5-3/4 inch push-in rod.

At some production facilities, front barrel bands drilled to accept the rod were installed, but the stocks were not drilled for the rod nor were the metal plugs installed. Substitute Type 99 rifles with welded front bands pinned to the barrel were not issued with any cleaning rod.

Dustcover and Dustcover Grooves

All early configuration Type 99 rifles were issued with dust covers numbered on the rear face to match the rifle's serial number. Mid-war, the dustcovers ceased to be included on new rifles, although receivers continued to have the two dustcover grooves machined into them. Only extremely late production rifles do not have dustcover grooves in the receiver.

Bore

Initially, the Type 99 was manufactured with a chrome bore to hinder corrosion. Most of these bores were still bright despite the use of corrosive ammunition during World War II, and can be identified by the bright chrome ring around the inside of the muzzle. Midway through the war the chrome lining was eliminated in new rifles.

The following tables indicate the production series during which major parts changes were introduced by each manufacturer. If a change occurred particularly early or late in a series, that is noted in parentheses.

Type 99 Parts

Nagoya Arsenal

Series	Parts Changes Introduced

Series   *Parts Changes Introduced*

None
- Oval rear sling swivel initially; later parallel sided swivel.

1-4
- All early configuration rifles.

5
- Two screw front band
- 4-7/8 inch cleaning rod
- Non-monopod rear band
- Dust cover eliminated (late)

6
- Rear ladder sight without anti-aircraft feature
- Grooved safety knob (late)
- Cylindrical bolt handle

7
- Short ladder rear sight
- Rough welded safety knob (late)
- Receiver marked only with chrysanthemum
- Substitute Type 99 with the following features (late):
    - Wood buttplate
    - Front sight without guards
    - Welded and pinned front band
    - Fixed peep sight
    - No cleaning rod
    - Short upper handguard
    - Large diameter recoil bolt

8
- Single screw rear sling swivel (early)
- Separate forestock
- Some rifles in the middle of this series were assembled with front sights having guards and receivers with Type 99 characters

10
- Continuation of late series 8 configuration

11
- Hole in stock for sling (late)
- Dust cover grooves eliminated from receiver

12
- Continuation of late series 11 configuration

Type 99 Parts

Kokura Arsenal

Series	Parts Changes Introduced

20-22
- All early configuration rifles

23
- 5-3/4" cleaning rod (late)

24
- 4-7/8" cleaning rod (early)
- Stocks not drilled for clearing rod (late)
- Non-monopod rear band
- Rear ladder sight without anti-aircraft feature
- Rough welded safety knob
- Dust cover eliminated (very early)
- Square recoil bolt (appears in middle of series)

25
- Receiver marked only with chrysanthemum
- Two screw front band
- Substitute Type 99 with the following features:
    - Wood buttplate (including a few double-thick)
    - Front sight without guards
    - Welded and pinned front band
    - Fixed peep sight
    - No cleaning rod
    - Short upper handguard
    - Large diameter recoil bolt
    - Rough welded safety knob
    - Oval bolt handle knob and two screw rear sling swivel were retained throughout production at Kokura Arsenal

Type 99 Parts

Toyo Kogyo

Series   *Parts Changes Introduced*

30-31   • All early configuration rifles

32   • Two screw front band
       • 4-7/8" cleaning rod
       • Non-monopod rear band
       • Rear ladder sight without anti-aircraft feature
       • Dust cover eliminated

33   • Smooth safety knob
       • Receiver marked only with chrysanthemum
       • Wood buttplate (late)
       • Front sight without guards

34   • Substitute Type 99 with the following features (mid-series):
            • Wood buttplate (including a few double-thick)
            • Front sight without guards
            • Welded and pinned front band
            • Fixed peep sight
            • No cleaning rod
            • Short upper handguard
            • Large diameter recoil bolt
            • Single screw rear swivel
            • Rough welded safety knob
            • Oval bolt handle knob was retained throughout production
                at Toyo Kogyo
            • Some rifles assembled on previously-rejected early-style
                stocks

35   • Continuation of late series 34 configuration

Type 99 Parts

Tokyo Juki Kogyo

Series	Parts Changes Introduced

27

- All rifles in this series have Substitute Type 99 features (receiver marked only with chrysanthemum, welded and pinned front band, fixed peep sight, no cleaning rod, and wood buttplate) although about the first 5,300 rifles were assembled on early stocks (inletted for early buttplates, 2-screw front bands, and 2-screw rear sling swivels), with short handguards. Late in the series the oval bolt handle was replaced with the cylindrical knob and a hole in the buttstock for a rope sling replaced the rear sling swivel.

37

- The initial 21,000 rifles in this series are early configuration with all typical early features. Throughout the rest of the series the following changes were introduced:
  - Receiver marked only with chrysanthemum
  - Non-monopod rear band
  - Front sight without guards
  - Rear ladder sight without the anti-aircraft feature
  - 2-screw front band without a rod
  - Wood buttplate

Izawa Jyuko

Series	Parts Changes Introduced

4

- Almost all early configuration rifles. The last few hundred rifles produced had non-monopod rear bands and rear sights without the anti-aircraft feature.

9

- The initial 7,000 rifles produced had all early configuration parts with the exception of 2-screw front bands and 4-7/8 inch rods, non-monopod rear bands, and rear sights without the anti-aircraft feature. The remainder of the series has Substitute Type 99 features with the exception of the front bands, which are either 2-screw or 1-screw, the latter being unique to this series.

Type 99 Parts

Howa Jyuko

Series | Parts Changes Introduced

9
- The initial 2,000 rifles produced had a combination of early and late features, including:
- Front sight with guards
- Two-screw front band
- Non-monopod rear band
- Rear ladder sight with or without anti-aircraft feature
- Small diameter recoil bolt
- Two-screw rear sling swivel
- Cupped metal buttplate
- The remaining production in the series consisted of Substitute Type 99 rifles.
- Hole in stock for sling (very late)

Jinsen Arsenal

Series | Parts Changes Introduced

40
- The initial 2,000-3,000 rifles in this series are early configuration with all early features. Thereafter a variety of parts changes were introduced, including:
- Cylindrical bolt handle
- Rear sight slide without the anti-aircraft feature
- Cylindrical bolt handle
- Large diameter recoil bolt
- Two-screw front band
- 4-7/8" rod
- Front sight without guards
- Receiver marked only with chrysanthemum
- Wood buttplate
- After about serial number 42,000 rifles are in the Substitute Type 99 configuration, many without dustcover grooves in the receiver.
- Beginning about serial number 82,000, three additional changes occur: a front band with a flat top; an extra-wide rear band; and a bolt release with a finger notch instead of the usual raised lip. Rifles with these three features have been termed by collectors as the Jinsen Special Last Ditch.

Type 2 Paratroop Rifle

The Imperial Japanese Army and Navy both instituted paratroop training programs in 1940 under German instructors. Rigid qualifications and short, but intense, training produced elite units in both services that were used in a small number of operations with little tactical success. Japanese parachutists were used in the capture of Palembang (Sumatra), Timor, and Celebes Island early in 1942; in Hunan, China in 1943 and 1944; and on Leyte in the Philippines in late 1944.

At the same time as special paratroop units were formed, the Army began development of specialized weapons that could be made short enough for a paratrooper to carry in a jump pack or special bag attached to his leg. Two types of rifles were made on an experimental basis by modifying existing weapons.

In 1940, Type 99 rifles from series 1, 21, and 22 were modified to separate into two sections at the chamber. Unofficially designated as the Type 100 rifle, the chamber of the barrel protruded rearward from the front section and fit into a matching hole in the front of the receiver on the rear section. The two sections were locked together with an interrupted thread arrangement, and separated by sliding a latch on the receiver bottom. The bolt handle was threaded into the bolt body and was removable.

The following year, 1941, a modified ver-

The characters for "2 Type" read from muzzle to breech, (top to bottom).

sion of the Type 38 carbine was tested. The modification consisted of cutting the stock through the wrist and installing a large hinge to allow the stock to be folded.

Not until 1942 was a suitable design developed, which was then finalized and adopted in 1943 as the Type 2 rifle. This rifle was a modification of the Type 99 design and separated at the chamber into two sections like the experimental Type 100. The sections were locked together with a tapered wedge that passed laterally through the joint area and mated with a notch machined in the bottom of the cham-

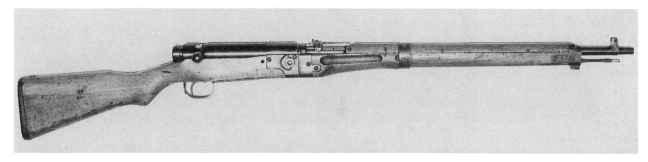

The Type 2 paratroop rifle was manufactured beginning in 1943. It separates into two parts at the breech for easier transport by parachute troops.

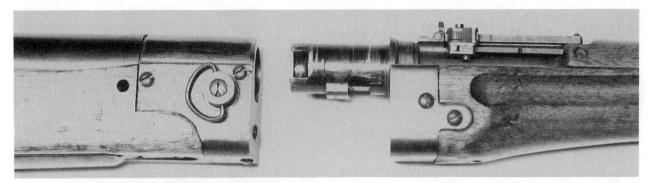

The chamber section of the Type 2 barrel inserts into the receiver and is held in place by a tapered wedge that fits against the block on the bottom of the chamber. The wedge is attached to a threaded sleeve that is loosened or tightened with the attached wire bail.

ber. The wedge was secured into the reinforcing band on the rifle's rear section by a large, rotating threaded head that was turned with the aid of an attached wire bail.

Approximately 22,000 Type 2 rifles were manufactured at Nagoya Arsenal beginning in late 1943. These rifles were similar to early transitional Type 99 rifles in their design features. All rifles had a full length handguard, dustcover, cupped metal buttplate, front sight with guards, oval-shaped bolt handle, knurled safety knob, non-monopod rear band, three-screw front band, two-screw rear sling swivel, 21-5/16 inch cleaning rod, and square cleaning rod release button.

Early production rifles had rear sights with the anti-aircraft feature, while later rifles had rear ladder sights without that feature. Early rifles had two drain holes in the stock; one on the right side at the front of the receiver, and the other on the bottom of the forward

Matching assembly numbers appear on the left side of both stock reinforcing bands, on the barrel below the sight, and on the receiver just behind the reinforcing band.

section immediately ahead of the connection area. On later production rifles these drain holes were eliminated.

A final feature of the Type 2 was a 1-5/8-inch by 1/2-inch groove in the stock above the rear sling swivel to facilitate the use of a quick release sling.

In addition to parts that are numbered to match the last three digits of the rifle serial number (bottom of the barrel chamber, bolt, safety, firing pin, extractor, dustcover and front band), an assembly number unrelated to the serial number appeared on the left side of the front and rear reinforcement bands in the joint area, on the left side of the barrel below the rear sight, on the left side of the receiver adjacent to the reinforcing band, and on the threaded wedge head.

Concentric Circle Rifles

A small number of Type 38 and Type 99 rifles had two concentric circles on the receiver in place of the chrysanthemum. The purpose of these specially-marked rifles is not known, although it is speculated that they were issued to paramilitary forces such as the Kempei Tai (Japanese Secret Police), other military police, and guards at prisons, embassies, and other civil installations.

Some concentric circle rifles were re-marked standard issue Type 38 and Type 99 rifles that had the chrysanthemum completely or partially removed and replaced with the concentric circle marking. These rifles were serialized separately from regular production pieces. Other rifles apparently were originally manufactured and marked with concentric circles.

Most concentric circle rifles were marked with two additional inspection stamps on various parts — the Arabic numeral 2 and a mark consisting of two horizontal lines enclosed in a circle, similar to the fourth series mark. It is unknown why concentric circle rifles had these additional inspection stamps. The Arabic 2, in particular, often appeared on parts such as screws that normally have no inspection stamps.

Concentric circle Type 38 rifles bear Nagoya and Koishikawa (Tokyo)/Kokura Arsenal marks. Many are also marked on the receiver with the school mark described earlier. The serial number range from Nagoya Arsenal is approximately 1-2,600,

The chrysanthemum was removed from this early configuration Type 99 rifle and the concentric circle mark stamped in its place.

and from the Koishikawa (Tokyo)/Kokura Arsenals approximately 1-2,800.

Perhaps as many as 5,300 concentric circle Type 99 rifles were manufactured at Nagoya Arsenal, Kokura Arsenal, and by Tokyo Juki Kogyo.

Many of those produced at Nagoya Arsenal had internal assembly numbers, but no external serial number. All Nagoya rifles were of the early configuration with monopods and anti-aircraft sight wings.

Tokyo Juki Kogyo rifles also were all early configuration, and had the second series *kana* mark preceding the serial number.

Kokura Arsenal produced two groups of Type 99 concentric circle rifles — an early configuration group, and a group with Substitute Type 99 features. The accompanying table illustrates approximate Type 99 serial number ranges.

Type 99 Concentric Circle Rifle Production

Manufacturer	Approx. Serial Numbers	Rifle Configuration
Nagoya Arsenal	1-600	Early
Nagoya Arsenal	(Assembly numbers 1-700)	Early
Tokyo Juki Kogyo	Series 2, 1-600	Early
Kokura Arsenal	1-1,400	Early
Kokura Arsenal	1,800-3,400	Late

Other Rifles

The Japanese used a variety of other rifles during World War II, which it is beyond the scope of this book to describe in detail. Some are so-called Last Ditch rifles, assembled late in the war as an emergency measure for the anticipated final battle for the home islands of Japan.

Others were manufactured in China to equip the millions of Japanese troops who fought there from 1937 to 1945. Large numbers of crudely-made training rifles were produced to familiarize future soldiers with basic firearms handling and drill. None of these rifles, except the trainers, are common, but several are briefly described.

Sniper Rifles

The Japanese used two primary sniper rifles during World War II: the Type 97, adopted in 1937, was a 6.5mm rifle similar to the Type 38 rifle; the Type 99 was a sniper version of the standard 7.7mm Type 99 rifle. Both models were manufactured as snipers, rather than converted from existing infantry rifles, although the quality of manufacture was no better than that of the standard infantry weapons.

Approximately 22,000 Type 97 and 12,000 Type 99 sniper rifles were manufactured at Nagoya Arsenal and Kokura Arsenal. Other than the addition of a telescopic sight, the main distinguishing feature of these rifles was a bolt handle that was longer than on standard infantry rifles and bent down to clear the scope when it was operated.

Type 97 rifles were fitted with a 2.5-power scope that fit in a dovetail mount on the left side of the receiver. The scopes were zeroed to individual rifles at the factory, numbered externally to match the rifle serial number, and had no external adjustments. Sighting was accomplished using the sight reticule, which was marked

Scopes on Type 97s were sighted to specific rifles at the factory and marked externally with the rifle's serial number. The locking lever rotates forward to release and rearward to lock the scope into place. For reasons that are unclear, matching rifles and scopes are almost never encountered.

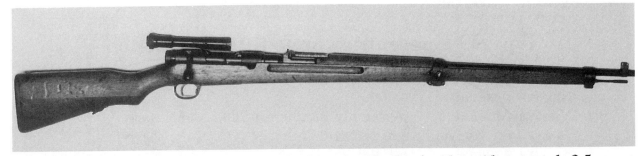

The Type 97 sniper rifle is essentially a Type 38-style rifle fitted with a side-mounted, 2.5 power telescopic sight. The rubber eye cup is missing from this example.

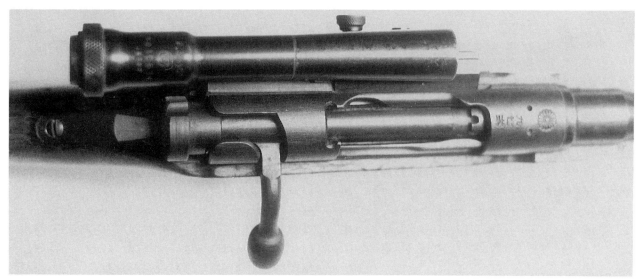

Scope tubes for Type 97 rifles were marked with the scope maker's mark and a manufacturer's serial number that is different from the rifle's serial number.

for different ranges and windage corrections.

Approximately 8,000 Type 97 rifles were produced at Kokura Arsenal and slightly over 14,000 produced at Nagoya Arsenal. Apparently all Kokura and about the first half of Nagoya rifles were equipped with a folding monopod similar to that used on the later Type 99 infantry rifles. This, in fact, was the first use of the rifle monopod by the Japanese. During the second half of production at Nagoya Arsenal, the rear barrel bands were not drilled for installation of monopods.

Type 99 sniper rifle development began in 1941, and included the same type of dovetail scope mount as the Type 97. Kokura Arsenal produced about 1,000 rifles, almost all equipped with a 2.5-power scope similar to that on the Type 97. Nagoya

Arsenal produced about 10,000 Type 99 sniper rifles. Those serial numbered between approximately 5,000 and 7,000 also were fitted with 2.5-power scopes; the balance had larger 4-power scopes.

These scopes also were zeroed to a specific rifle at the factory, and numbered on the dovetail with the rifle serial number. On a small number of 4-power scopes the scope tube could be adjusted externally within the mounting rings to align it with the rifle's barrel. Even these scopes did not have calibrated external windage and range adjustments, but were sighted using reticule range and windage markings.

Type 99 sniper rifles were fitted with non-monopod rear bands, short screw-in cleaning rods, and rear ladder sights with or without anti-aircraft sight wings attached. This configuration conforms to the initial

The Type 99 sniper rifle was not officially adopted as a new rifle model and retained the designation of the infantry rifle from which it was adopted. The rubber eye cup on this example is a modern reproduction.

The Type 99 scope attachment mechanism is similar to that on the Type 97 sniper. Scopes were sighted to individual rifles, but were numbered with the rifle's serial number on the inside of the mounting dovetail, rather than externally.

simplification of the Type 99 rifle prior to the adoption of the Substitute Type 99 rifle in 1943.

Scopes for Type 97 and Type 99 sniper rifles were issued in hard canvas carrying cases with shoulder straps. Early issue cases for Type 97 scopes were made of leather.

Scopes were produced by several private manufacturers. The top of the scope tubes were marked with the manufacturer's symbol and the manufacturer's serial number. These serial numbers are different from the rifle serial numbers found on the mounting portions of the scopes.

Most Type 99 scopes were 4 power. The top of the tube is marked with the manufacturer's mark and serial number.

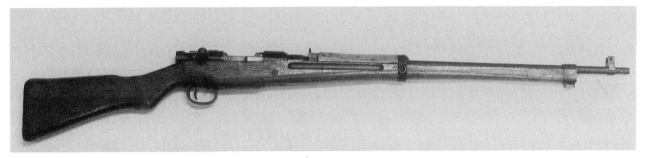

The Naval Special Type 99 was a "last ditch" rifle manufactured for Imperial Japanese Navy use.

Naval Special Type 99 Rifle

About 14,000 of these rifles were manufactured for Imperial Japanese Navy use during World War II, and had several unique features. Although the basic design followed the Type 99 rifle, the Naval Special Type 99 had many cast iron parts, including the receiver. It also had a one-piece buttstock, and usually was marked on the receiver with a naval anchor instead of the imperial chrysanthemum.

Early production rifles had oval-shaped bolt handles, full length handguards, non-monopod rear bands, adjustable ladder rear sights, front sights with guards, and knurled safety knobs. Early receivers were marked with a *kanji* character for "special" and the characters for "99 Type," as well as the naval anchor.

Late production rifles had cylindrical bolt handles, short handguards, fixed rear peep sights, front sights without guards, rough welded safety knobs, and no wrist tangs. Although there were no arsenal marks on these rifles, it is believed that they were manufactured at Yokosuka Naval Arsenal.

Type 02/45 Rifle

Late in the war, an unknown number of rifles were assembled using Type 35 rifle receivers and bolts, 6.5mm rifle or (rarely) machine gun barrels, and training rifle stocks and other parts. The Type 35 rifle was adopted by the Japanese Navy in 1902 and manufactured in small numbers. The actions used for the Type 02/45 rifles apparently were left over from that period of manufacture and had characters for "35 Year Type" and the imperial chrysanthemum on the top of the receiver. The type designation "02/45" is a creation of collectors to reflect the 1902 adoption of the action and the presumed 1945 assembly of

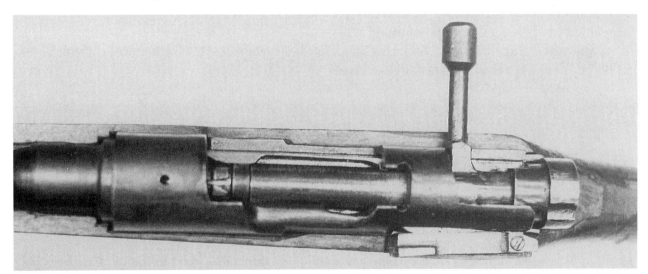

The slightly oversized receiver of the Naval Special Type 99 rifle is made of cast iron. The bolt locks into the barrel chamber rather than the receiver.

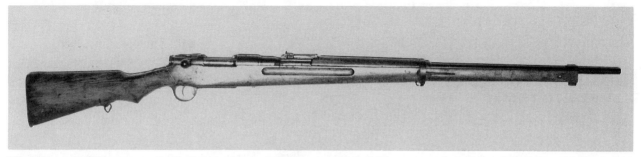

The Type 02/45 was a crude late war expedient assembled from stored, unserialized Type 35 actions and trainer rifle stocks and parts. The Type 02/45 designation was created by collectors to reflect the year the receivers were adopted (1902) and the year these rifles were assembled (1945).

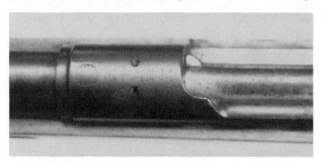

The markings on the receiver top read, from the muzzle to the breech (left to right), "3 10 5 Year Type." These markings were put on the receivers when they were originally manufactured for Type 35 rifles.
these rifles.

North China Type 19 Carbine

In 1944 and 1945 a variation of the Type 38 carbine was manufactured in several captured Chinese arsenals. Although chambered for the 6.5mm cartridge, it differed from the standard Type 38 carbine by having no top handguard, a one-piece buttstock, and a front band attached with a single lateral screw. Its receiver was stamped with the Japanese characters for "North China 19 Type," and with a five-petalled flower that appears on some other rifles of Chinese manufacture. The Type 19 designation apparently refers to 1944, the nineteenth year of the Showa era.

Based on reported serial numbers, several thousand of these carbines were made in three or four different Chinese facilities. Serial numbers appeared on the left side of the receiver, followed by a Chinese arsenal mark. Early production rifles had an adjustable ladder rear sight, sling swivels, wrist tangs, finger grooves in the stock, blued finish, and a cross-hatched pattern on the safety knob face.

Late production rifles had a fixed peep rear sight, no sling swivels, no wrist tangs, no finger grooves, blued or black paint

北 支 一 九 式

These characters read, left to right, "North China 1 9 Type."

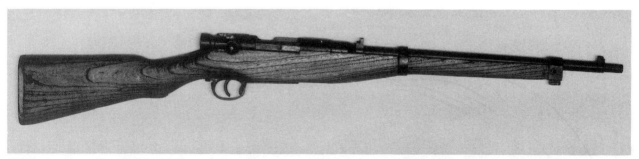

This very late North China Type 19 carbine has a one-piece buttstock, wood buttplate, fixed rear peep sight, no sling swivels or wrist tangs, and black paint finish on all metal parts. The most distinctive features of these rifles are the "pot bellied" stock behind the rear band, and the lack of a top handguard.

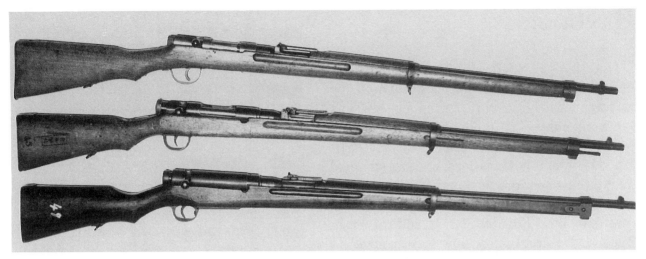

Shown are three of the many varieties of Japanese training rifles. They are, from top, a non-firing "clicker" with a large-diameter plunger in the bolt rather than a firing pin; a single-loading smoothbore, styled after the Type 38 rifle; and a magazine-loading smoothbore, styled after the Type 99 long rifle.

metal finish, a smooth safety knob face, and a wood buttplate.

Training Rifles

The Japanese used a wide variety of training rifles during World War II, mostly for students and home defense units. These rifles often resembled Type 38 or Type 99 rifles, but were poorly made and not usually intended for firing regular ammunition. Training rifles frequently had one-piece buttstocks, smoothbore barrels, and large characters burned or pressed into the side of the buttstock.

Some had magazines and were intended to fire blank ammunition, while others were single shot or not intended to fire any ammunition. There were a variety of receiver marks, although many guns were unmarked. Crudely-made training bayonets with dull edges were issued for use with training rifles.

Standard issue rifles also were converted to training rifles. Prior to the early 1920s, about 10,000 Type 30 "hook safety" rifles were converted to smooth bore trainers and marked on their receivers with characters for "blank ammunition only." Numbers of Type 38 rifles also were withdrawn from service for use as trainers. Generally, the chrysanthemum was canceled, the "school" mark (see page 13) added to the receiver, and two or three zeros added to the front of the serial number.

Bayonets

The bayonet used on all Arisaka rifles, except the Type 44 carbine, was the Type 30 bayonet originally designed for the Type 30 "hook safety" rifle adopted in 1897. This bayonet featured a 15-5/8" blue or bright finished blade with fullers, contoured wood grip panels secured with two screws, a contoured bird's head pommel, a muzzle ring, and a hooked quillon. The standard scabbard had a steel body and was secured to the soldier's belt with a leather frog.

Bayonets were made by at least 13 different manufacturers, including Nagoya Arsenal, Koishikawa (Tokyo) Arsenal, Kokura Arsenal, Jinsen Arsenal, Mukden Arsenal, and various private subcontractors. The maker's mark appeared on the right ricasso of the blade. Usually a serial number was stamped on the end of the pommel. Except possibly for extremely early production, it is not believed that bayonet serial numbers were intended to match rifle serial numbers.

During World War II, the manufacture of bayonets was simplified in the same fashion as that of Type 99 rifles. Design modifications included a straight crossguard instead of a hooked quillon, unfullered blade, simplified contours or uncontoured

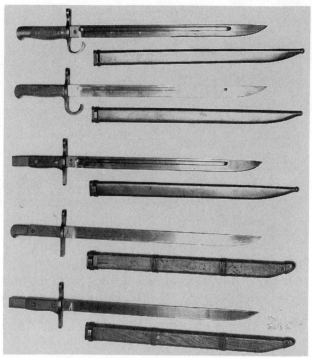

These bayonets range from pre-war, top, to late war configurations. The scabbards with the two late bayonets, bottom, are made of wood wrapped with twine or wire and have metal end fittings.

grips and pommel, grip panels secured by rivets rather than screws, and wooden scabbards held together with wire or twine wrappings and having steel throats and tips.

Bayonet frogs, originally made of leather, later were manufactured from layers of canvas impregnated with latex and pressed together (referred to as "rubberized canvas"), or from heavy canvas.

Slings

Arisaka rifles can be found with several types of slings. Prior to World War II, leather slings were standard issue. Japanese slings generally had a single, large square or rectangular buckle, a two-headed button attachment at the front end, and one or two keepers.

Most commonly encountered are slings for the Type 38 rifle (1-1/8 inches wide and approximately 43 inches long); the Type 38 carbine (1-1/8 inches wide and 40 inches or less in length); and the Type 99 rifle (1-3/8 inches wide and approximately 40 inches long).

As with bayonet frogs, belts, ammunition pouches, pistol holsters, and other equipment normally made of leather, during World War II the Japanese used rubberized canvas for rifle slings. These slings generally conformed to the dimensions of Type 99 leather slings. Other varieties of wartime sling production or use included heavy webbed canvas with wire loops at each end, canvas, and braided rope or palm fronds.

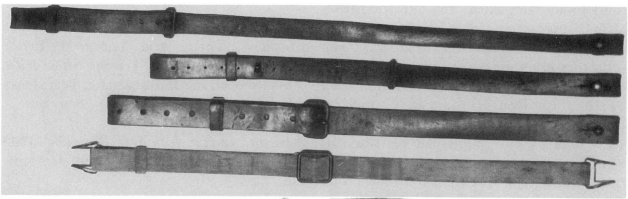

Rifle slings, from top: leather Type 38 rifle, leather Type 38 carbine, leather Type 99 rifle, and heavy webbed canvas with wire loops at each end.

Late war sling expedients included braided rope, top, and braided palm leaves, bottom.

Author's Note on Sources

This volume is intended to provide collectors with an up-to-date introduction to Japanese military rifles used during World War II. It would not have been possible without the original research and comprehensive publications of others.

The groundbreaking work in this field was *Military Rifles of Japan* by Fred L. Honeycutt and F. Patt Anthony, now in its 4th edition. *Military Rifles of Japan* is the source of much of the historical information, production data, and interpretation of markings included in the present volume. It is an essential source for advanced collectors of Japanese rifles.

The *Banzai* newsletter was started in 1982 by the late Don Harper, continued by Kathleen Harper-White until her death in 1994, and is now published by Doss H. White Jr. This outstanding monthly publication contains a wealth of information on Japanese military weapons, equipment, and history in the form of articles by subscribers. It has served as a catalyst for many research projects by members, and as a means of disseminating information about Japanese militaria. Much information on weapons variations and production ranges in this work has come from the pages of *Banzai*.

Especially valuable have been two ongoing *Banzai* research projects: Type 99 rifle research coordinated by Doss H. White Jr., and Type 38 rifle and carbine research coordinated by the late Harold W. Macy.

The Japanese Type 99 Arisaka Short Rifle by Doss H. White, Jr., et al. is a publication that resulted from the Type 99 research conducted through the medium of *Banzai*. It contains detailed serial number tables on Type 99 rifles and is the source of additional parts variation information in the present book.

Collectors interested in further information on Japanese rifles and bayonets are encouraged to consult the following sources:

Honeycutt, Fred L., Jr. and F. Patt Anthony, *Military Rifles of Japan*. 4th ed., 1993, Julin Books, Palm Beach Gardens, FL.

Banzai newsletter, 1982-present, 4001 Windermere Drive, Tuscaloosa, AL 35403

White, Doss H., Jr., William S. White, Frank A. Knapp, and George H. Taylor, *The Japanese Type 99 Arisaka Short Rifle*. 1985, Shoestring Publications, Tuscaloosa, AL.

Johnson, Larry, *Japanese Bayonets*. 1988, Cedar Ridge Publications, Broken Arrow, OK.

McLean, Donald B., ed., *Japanese Parachute Troops*. 1973, Normount Technical Publications, Wickenburg, AZ.

Bruderlin, Lt. Edward B. and Lt. Robert S. Nelson, *Ordnance Technical Intelligence Report Number 19*. 13 March 1946, Office of the Chief Ordnance Officer, General Headquarters, Army Forces, Pacific, Tokyo, Japan (Reprinted 1971 in the United States).

Two books containing extensive analyses of Japanese rifles by World War II veterans who also were firearms experts are:

Dunlop, Roy F., *Ordnance Went Up Front*. 1948, Thomas G. Samworth (Reprinted 1993 by R & R Books).

George, Lt. Col. John, *Shots Fired in Anger.* 2nd ed. 1981, National Rifle Association, Washington, DC.

Other sources consulted are:

Derby, III, Harry L., *The Hand Cannons of Imperial Japan.* 1981, Derby Publishing Company, Charlotte, NC.

Packard, Jerrold, M., *Sons of Heaven: A Portrait of the Japanese Monarchy.* 1987, Charles Scribner's Sons, New York.

Venturoli, Ugo, "Type 'I' Not 'Made in Japan,'" *American Rifleman,* December, 1971, pp. 62-63.

Wiley, Peter Booth, *Yankees in the Land of the Gods: Commodore Perry and the Opening of Japan.* 1990, Viking Penguin, New York.

Acknowledgments

This book was suggested by my publisher, Al Petrillo of Excalibur Publications, without whose patient encouragement it would not have been completed.

I am greatly indebted to the many contributors to the *Banzai* newsletter, whose articles have enhanced our knowledge of Japanese militaria for well over a decade.

Peter and Masumi McCollum answered numerous questions about the reading and meaning of Japanese characters.

Special thanks go to Bobby Blevins, the late Harold W. Macy, and Doss H. White Jr. for their many valuable comments on a draft of this book. They pointed out errors and made insightful observations that were incorporated into the text.

I am grateful to Bobby Blevins, Michael Morrissey, Steven Vallejo, Doss H. White Jr., and an anonymous collector for permission to photograph items in their collections to illustrate this book. All photos were taken by the author, except the view of the Naval Special Type 99 on page 53, which was taken by Alan M. Petrillo.

About the Author

Duncan McCollum is a professional records manager and archivist and avid student of military history. Born on the island of Saipan, he has long had an interest in the Pacific War and in Japanese militaria. His other interests include Japanese history, the history of the American West, and camping and hiking with his family in the mountains of Colorado.